Just as the Warrens were to leave—the limousine being readied in a nearby garage—Lorraine looked out the window and saw on the moon-silvered parade grounds a genuine apparition—

—a black man dressed in a turn-of-the-century uniform without braids or insignia of any kind (as if all privilege had been stripped away from him) standing sadly looking up at Thayer house.

This was the angry presence Lorraine had instinctively known about all day long.

Who are you?

(Still gazing up at her.) My name is Greer.

You are troubled.

(He helped her form an image in her mind: a small, cell-like room . . . where he seemed to be confined.) I am not free.

What happened to you?

(An overwhelming sense of sorrow. Greer, in his stripped-bare uniform, raised his sad eyes to Lorraine's, and then vanished.)

Greer, she wanted to say, Greer—I can help you.

But he was gone; gone.

Also by Ed and Lorraine Warren
with Robert Curran and Jack and Janet Smurl

THE HAUNTING

ED and LORRAINE WARREN
with ROBERT DAVID CHASE

Ghost Hunters

True Stories from the World's
Most Famous Demonologists

Futura

A **Futura** Book

Copyright © 1989 by Ed Warren, Lorraine Warren
and Robert David Chase
The right of Ed Warren, Lorraine Warren and
Robert David Chase to be identified as authors of
this work has been asserted.

First published in the USA in 1989
by St Martin's Press

First published in Great Britain in 1990
by Futura Publications, a Division of
Macdonald & Co (Publishers) Ltd
London & Sydney
Reprinted 1991

ISBN 0 7088 4837 0

Printed and bound in Great Britain by
HarperCollins Manufacturing, Glasgow

Futura Publications
A Division of
Macdonald & Co (Publishers) Ltd
165 Great Dover Street
London SE1 4YA

A member of Maxwell Macmillan Publishing Corporation

Contents

GHOST
HUNTERS

INTRODUCTION

IT was not the type of story you expected to find in *The New York Times*. Nor was it the type of story you expected to find coming from America's most prestigious military institution, West Point.

Yet for four days, newspapers and television newscasts and radio shows around the world carried breaking stories of demonic infestation at West Point—"demonic infestation" being a gentler way of saying "ghosts."

In the center of this unfolding tale—which many government officials hoped would soon go away—was a middle-age married couple named Ed and

Lorraine Warren. What made the pair so interesting to reporters was their occupation. They were demonologists, people who had dedicated their lives to the study of the supernatural and the occult.

Yet "study" is perhaps too passive a word, for it implies that the Warrens spent most of their time poring through dusty volumes filled with ancient and macabre lore.

In fact, the Warrens have traveled worldwide, participating in every kind of supernatural activity, from watching violent phantoms hurl axes at living human beings, to assisting priests in the rites of exorcism.

Long before the world press "discovered" them at West Point, Ed and Lorraine were well known to a variety of people needing their help—from police detectives, for whom Lorraine's psychic powers have helped solve murders, to movie stars concerned that their homes may be haunted.

Many times their lives have been in jeopardy. Many times they have found themselves trapped in the clutches of the spirit realm. Many times they have been forced to help people whom authorities of all kinds—governmental, medical, and religious—have abandoned.

So who are these people who helped West Point understand its ghost problems?

Both in their sixties, the Warrens have been married for more than forty years. Ed is currently director of the New England Society of Psychic Research. His interest in demonology dates back to childhood, when the house he was raised in proved to be haunted. As a child, he saw objects flying around his house many times. He has even seen apparitions, people appearing to him.

Lorraine's experience with the paranormal also began at an early age. As a girl, she saw lights around people's heads. Later she understood these lights to be auras. She had a similar experience when she met Ed: "The night I was introduced to him, I saw a sixteen-year-old athletic young man standing in front of me but then I flashed forward, glimpsed the future and saw a heavier, graying man, and I knew this was Ed at a future date. I also knew that I would spend my entire life with him."

Ed and Lorraine met during World War II. Ed went to art school, while Lorraine was a self-taught artist. Their daughter, Judy, was born while Ed was still in the service. Later they traveled around the countryside in a '33 Chevrolet Daisy with a German shepherd in the backseat. "We like to think of ourselves as the first hippies," Ed has said humorously.

"But our interest in hauntings and demonology remained constant. People are always surprised at how closely the supernatural and the occult brush against their lives. Many cases of so-called mental illness are really the result of possession. Many cases of murder are likewise the result of demon possession. From the start, we were determined to investigate every peculiar happening we heard of.

"Over the years we gathered a reputation as serious students of such occurrences. Through all our exposure to demons, we also began to learn how to deal with them."

In recent years the Warrens were involved in perhaps the most celebrated case of demonic infestation in the United States: Amityville. While they express displeasure with the fact that "many things were exaggerated or left out of [the] book," they see the Amityville story as making believers of many former skeptics.

Their fame has continued to spread. Three books have been written about them—*Deliver Us From Evil* by Gerald Sawyer, *The Devil in Connecticut* by Gerald Brittle, and *The Demonologist*, also by Brittle. They also figured prominently in *The Haunted*, a terrifying ongoing example of demonic infestation that is updated in this book. In addition, hundreds of articles and two television shows of their own have further brought the Warrens to public attention. A few years ago NBC made a TV movie based on one of the Warrens' cases. Even academia has beckoned; Ed and Lorraine have taught courses on demonology at Southern Connecticut State University.

The Warrens state: "We have a single message we want to get across to the public—that there is a demonic underworld and that on some occasions it can be a terrifying problem for people."

That demonic underworld, the Warrens tell us, is composed of both human and inhuman spirits. Human spirits, which once walked the earth as individuals, can be either positive or negative in intent. In contrast, inhuman spirits never had a corporeal existence, but instead roam the earth through oppression or possession of a human spirit. These inhuman spirits can represent elemental (or natural) forces, demonic powers, or even the devil.

Ghost Hunters contains some of the Warrens' most frightening and baffling investigations. Here you will meet, among many others, a thirteen-year-old girl sexually ravaged by a demon; a small American town put under a spell by satanic forces; a movie star who senses that a dark fate awaits her in a certain house; and the legendary creature Bigfoot, with whom the Warrens had a near-tragic encounter in a shadowy forest.

Ghost Hunters offers irrefutable proof that the "demonic underworld" Ed speaks of actually exists—and plays a far more prominent role in our daily lives than most of us would like to admit.

And you can ask the people at West Point about that. While interest in that particular story gradually waned, you'll find full details of the case here—a story that Point officials, while not exactly confirming, could not deny.

Shocking, alarming, and unnerving as these tales may be, the Warrens have lived them and know them to be true.

Join us now on a journey through nightmare, in the experienced capable hands of the world's most celebrated demonologists, Ed and Lorraine Warren.

Case File:

WEST POINT

THERE is no institution in the United States more highly regarded than West Point in New York State. Founded in 1802, after George Washington himself had suggested such an academy, West Point has a history unmatched by any other such institution in the world.

Its graduates include such famous leaders as Stonewall Jackson, Robert E. Lee, and Dwight David Eisenhower.

"The Point," as it is called by its graduates, has a well-deserved reputation for producing men and women whose training has

*taught them to be hardheaded realists not
given to flights of fancy. So you can imagine
what it was like for Lorraine and me to be
told—by some of these hardheaded realists
themselves—that ghosts were haunting certain
of the buildings at The Point. . . .*

*The year was 1972. At the time, Lorraine
and I had a manager named Cindy De Sano
who helped us schedule our speaking engagements. Before hearing anything about ghosts
at West Point, Cindy had scheduled us to
speak there at the request of staff and students
alike. We were flattered. Like most Americans, we have great respect for our military
academies. So it was a special thrill to be
asked by such a group to tell them about
ourselves and our work.*

*We accepted the invitation at once and
were told that on the appointed day, a military
car would pick us up at our home.*

*Few speaking engagements make us
nervous—we've become accustomed to sharing
ourselves with audiences of every kind—but
both of us admitted to a little bit of apprehen-
sion as the day approached.*

This was, after all, West Point.

—Ed Warren

Lorraine smiled to herself when she saw the
"car" that had been dispatched from West Point.
This sort of limousine was something she had seen
previously only in movies. Dark, sleek, formidable,

it seemed out of place pulling up before the modest home the Warrens had built earlier in the year.

She could tell from Ed's expression that he felt the same way—a little bit stunned, a little bit intimidated.

A tall, ramrod-straight driver in an army uniform emerged from the limousine. He held the door for them and they got inside, still exchanging nervous glances.

Over the next few hours, they passed through some of the most beautiful land in the nation, rural hills and valleys fiery with hot October autumn. The limousine's motor hummed without flaw; the air-conditioning system kept them cool. The deep leather seats seemed almost to swaddle them in comfort and luxury. Only when he was spoken to did the driver say anything. Otherwise, he kept both hands on the wheel and his eyes straight ahead. Lorraine marveled at the man's military bearing. If this was an example of West Point training, she was impressed.

As the limousine topped a hill, Lorraine caught her first glimpse of the military academy. She literally caught her breath. She had rarely seen anything so beautiful.

Set on part of a 16,000-acre military reservation and situated on the bank of the Hudson River in New York, West Point gives the impression of being a vast fortress of stone, brick, and mortar isolated from all civilization. In fact, the academy is only fifty miles from New York City.

The new visitor to The Point is first drawn to

Washington Hall, a huge building in front of which sprawls the main parade ground.

As the limousine drove onto the grounds that day, Lorraine was overwhelmed by a sense of history. American flags snapped in the soft breeze; cadets in perfect formation marched by. Taking Ed's hand, she knew he felt the same way.

The first part of the Warrens' visit was given over to a tour led by Major Dean Dowling. The Warrens got to see firsthand how West Point had evolved—from a few buildings to the gigantic complex of the present.

Throughout the tour, Major Dowling, another example of West Point bearing, asked the Warrens many questions about their work. He seemed particularly interested in their work with ghosts.

They soon were to learn why.

When they had finished the tour, Major Dowling asked the Warrens if they would accompany him to superintendent George Nolton's residence. At The Point, the superintendent is always an army lieutenant general who is in charge of the entire 16,000 acres, the military post, and the academy.

Nolton's residence was the Colonel Sylvanus Thayer home (Thayer had been the West Point superintendent from 1817 to 1833). A Federal-style house of white-painted brick, at first it looked appealing to Lorraine.

But as she drew close—and even before Major Dowling began to talk about the problems associated with the house—Lorraine began to tremble slightly and hear the distant but unmistakable keening of troubled spirits, a keening that often rings in the ears of gifted psychics.

Major Dowling was forthcoming. As they entered the house, he told them of many strange incidents that had taken place there over the past year. Many eyewitnesses had seen a bed stripped down by invisible hands. After being made again, an unseen force would once more strip it a few minutes later. For this reason alone, certain people at the academy made a point of avoiding the Thayer house, however urgent their business with General Nolton.

But there were even more troubling problems.

During their many years of investigating the occult and the supernatural, the Warrens had often encountered examples of "apports." In most cases, apports are objects that prove the presence of supernatural beings.

Major Dowling showed the Warrens a bread board. In the center of the wooden board was a wet spot approximately the size of a slice of bread. No matter how often the board was dried—nor no matter what method was used for drying it—the wet spot remained. And had remained for many months.

Upon seeing the bread board, Lorraine knew for sure that the sensations she was feeling—slight chills, the distant keening sound, the strange play of light and shadow in corners of the house—indicated that they were in the presence of supernatural entities. For proof positive of this, Major Dowling told them of apparitions seen not only by General Nolton and his wife but by overnight guests as well.

The litany of proof was familiar to Lorraine and Ed. Ghosts had demonstrated their presence not only by showing themselves but by knocking on walls and slamming doors and—perhaps most embarrassing—going through the personal belongings of guests. Everything from wallets and jewelry had been lifted and set down in some other part of the house. Clothes were torn from hangers and ripped from drawers.

There could be no doubt.

General Nolton's residence had been infested by ghosts. Their exact nature and purpose had yet to be determined.

An hour later Lorraine began to move through the house, room by room, and attempted to make contact with the ghosts that the general and his friends had seen. While not every attempt to contact the realm of the spirits is successful, Lorraine felt confident that with her background she could find out what was going on.

Her optimism, however, was soon quelled; the first three rooms yielded nothing—no response whatsoever from the spirits. She came to suspect that Major Dowling might doubt her special talents.

The process was the same in each room. Lorraine stood in the center of the room and "listened" through various means for any evidence of psychic activity. None.

In the fourth room, a surprise awaited her. She sat down in a lovely rocking chair and closed her eyes. Immediately she began experiencing the increased heartbeat and aural sensations that often accompany contact with ghosts.

Inexplicably, she began to feel a pressure on her arm, as if someone were gently prodding her. She knew now that there was definitely a supernatural presence in this room, but what she saw was so startling she was almost reluctant to reveal it.

To one of the major's aides, she said, "Would you happen to know if President Kennedy was ever in this room?"

The aide looked surprised. "Why, yes," he said. "This was the room he stayed in when he came to The Point."

Now Lorraine knew her emanation had been a valid one. She had not only sensed but glimpsed the image of President Kennedy, standing next to her, touching her gently on the shoulder so she would look up and see him. Long an admirer of the slain President, Lorraine felt an overwhelming sorrow during her last moments in the chair, the same rocker that John Fitzgerald Kennedy, with his well-known back problem, had also sat in.

After leaving the room where Kennedy had slept, Lorraine felt she might have solved the identity of the West Point ghost. But as she walked down the wide, sun-splashed hallway, she felt new emanations, far more troubling than the ones that had accompanied President Kennedy's image.

No, there were other ghosts in this venerable house. Her job was not done.

"The moment I walked into the master bedroom," Lorraine Warren revealed later, "I knew that this house was being troubled by a female presence. At the time, that was all I knew, but after half an hour in the room, I realized a lot more."

With Lorraine and Ed, plus Major Dowling and his aide, crowded into the master bedroom, the investigation centered on various china pieces and statues in the room, many dating from the Revolutionary War period.

"As I touched the pieces, I began to get a confusing signal," Lorraine explained. "The china that dated back two hundred years gave me no specific emanations at all—but there was new china and statuary that painted for me a picture of a very domineering, strong-willed woman.

"I left the room for a time and began walking around the rest of the house. The image of the domineering woman stayed with me, and I came to realize that it was she who troubled the air here— she who had unmade the beds and tossed personal belongings around in the guest rooms."

In a small, ancillary room, Lorraine stood for a time while the woman's presence filled the doorway. "I knew that the woman was a jealous, possessive spirit who felt the house belonged to her and who resented anybody else who lived here. This was not a dangerous spirit, but it was a troublesome one.

"I went back to the room I'd been in and told the major's aide what I'd discovered. 'Many pieces of china here belonged to a very strong-willed woman. Is that correct?'"

Startled, the aide revealed that between marriages, General Douglas MacArthur's wife had lived here. An insecure and somewhat angry woman, she took her supreme task to be running Thayer's house as it had never been run before. Servants feared her; even officers wilted before her stern presence.

The presence of a second spirit was thus explained . . . as was some of the more troubling behavior that had gone on in this house over the past year.

Still, as Lorraine walked around, she became aware of another presence—this one the true source of the icy chills she'd felt from time to time during the day.

JFK had been a most friendly spirit; Mrs. Mac-Arthur, while meddlesome, was also essentially benign, given over to pranks but nothing more dangerous.

But something else was in the air . . .

Lorraine sensed . . . violence.

She continued to move around the house, taking

time in each room to touch furnishings and aged woodwork polished to a fine shine.

The sense of . . . violence . . . did not leave her.

Something terrible had happened here—

And somebody who had been involved in the violence still roamed the hall, still hid in the dusky shadows of each chill room.

But, having nothing more specific to go on than her intuition, Lorraine relented and accompanied the rest of the group to the dining hall, where they would have a feast the finest restaurant would be proud to serve.

After that, Ed and Lorraine spent a long evening addressing the West Point audience, officers and spouses as well as cadets.

The Warrens found the group not only fascinated with their talk and their slides that showed proof of various types of supernatural activity; they also were more than willing to take such phenomena seriously.

At the end of the evening, several officers and their wives asked the Warrens if they would be willing to return to Thayer house and try to contact the spirits Lorraine had described.

Puzzled and dismayed by the angry presence she had sensed in the house, Lorraine was only too willing to agree.

In the master bedroom, the men and women sat on the floor in a semicircle around the bed. The officers opened the collars of their uniforms as Lorraine closed her eyes and began the difficult and occasionally frightening process of contacting earth's other realm.

Almost immediately, Lorraine felt great energy surge through the room, a certain sign that a spirit was present. She knew at once that Mrs. MacArthur was here. Lorraine, who happened to be sitting on the edge of the bed that Mrs. MacArthur had slept in, began to see the woman clearly. Everything she had assumed that afternoon about the woman—that here was a great, insecure tyrant of a woman whose presence was meant to challenge Lorraine's right to be there—was confirmed.

But Lorraine's strong will soon enough banished Mrs. MacArthur, and for the next half hour, the people from The Point and the Warrens enjoyed a pleasant discussion of the supernatural.

According to Ed, "It was really exciting, watching the future leaders of our country sitting there on the floor, dressed in their military garb, asking questions of us. There was no embarrassment whatsoever. Some of them had known, along with Lorraine and me, when Mrs. MacArthur's presence had come into the room. They had many more questions then about how to contact the other realm themselves."

The evening concluded with some of the guests getting the Warrens' address so they could get further information on the subject of the supernatural.

Lorraine had never felt better about the skills she and Ed had shared for so many years.

But just as the Warrens were to leave—the limousine being readied in a nearby garage—Lorraine looked out the window and saw on the moon-silvered parade grounds a genuine apparition:

—a black man dressed in a turn-of-the-century uniform without braids or insignia of any kind (as if all privilege had been stripped away from him) standing sadly looking up at Thayer house.

This was the angry presence Lorraine had known about instinctively all day long.

Who are you?

(Still gazing up at her.) My name is Greer.

You are troubled.

(He helped her form an image in her mind: a small, cell-like room, where he seemed to be confined.) I am not free.

What happened to you?

(An overwhelming sense of sorrow. Greer, in his stripped-bare uniform, raised his sad eyes to Lorraine's and then vanished.)

Greer (she wanted to say), Greer—I can help .you.

But he was gone, gone.

As the Warrens waited for their limousine in the soft smoky warmth of the autumn evening, Lorraine

told one of the aides about Greer. She described the
uniform but the aide shook his head. "There weren't
any black people at The Point at that time."

Troubled, Lorraine and Ed went home.

The adventure at The Point was to have two
endings, actually.

A week later the aide Lorraine had shared her
Greer story with called to say that he'd done some
research and that there had, in fact, been a black
man at The Point during the era Lorraine described.
His name was indeed Greer, and he had killed
another man there. Although guilty of the murder,
Greer was cleared by a military court and exoner-
ated.

As soon as the aide revealed this, Lorraine
recognized Greer for what he was—an angry, sad
spirit who could not accept his own guilt and therefore roamed The Point scaring people without really
meaning to. People sensed his rage—most likely
rage with himself for what he'd done—and were
frightened by it.

Thus the troubled spirit had been identified and
explained. The people at West Point were grateful
for what the Warrens had done.

Then came the second ending. Thanks to a navy
leak meant to embarrass the army, *The New York
Times* printed a story about ghosts at West Point.

Soon papers around the world were running the piece.

The Warrens, mentioned prominently in all press reports, found themselves celebrities. Their speaking engagements doubled in number, and TV shows that had shown little interest in them previously now came pleading for interviews.

Lorraine Warren laughs when she recalls the incident. "We met a lot of wonderful people at The Point, some of whom remain good friends until this very day. But you know what I never got over? The limousine. Believe me, it was wonderful!"

Case File:

MURDER MOST VIOLENT

DURING the past decades, Lorraine has been asked by several police departments to help identify and track down killers. But of all the cases, perhaps the most difficult for her involved a beautiful young woman who had only recently become a mother. Lorraine still has nightmares about the case, one so grisly in detail that time seems unable to dim its terrible reality.

—*Ed Warren*

April 2

Lorraine and Ed frequently spoke to classes at colleges (Ed and Lorraine have been cited as the most popular speakers by several national organizations). On this occasion, several members of the faculty were particularly interested in parapsychological phenomena and found that their students made especially rapt audiences for the Warrens.

On this rainy Southern day, as early flowers were just beginning to bud, Lorraine and Ed stood in front of a classroom showing slides that depicted various hauntings they had encountered over the years. In the course of the presentation, Lorraine noticed an older man, dressed in a snap-brim hat and a rain-dripping trench coat, walk quietly into the room and lean against the wall, watching the slide with a great deal of interest. He appeared to be neither student nor professor.

After the class ended, and many of the students drifted to the Warrens to ask further questions, the man came forward and took a desk seat. He waited patiently while the Warrens dealt with the students, rarely taking his solemn blue eyes off Lorraine.

When the final student had left, and the Warrens were packing up their slide trays, the man came forward and introduced himself.

"I'm Detective Joseph Steinberg," the man said. "I wondered if I could talk to you about a case I'm working on."

"Of course," Lorraine said, noticing how troubled—even grim—the detective seemed.

Fifteen minutes later, in the student lounge, Detective Steinberg outlined the difficulty he had been having with a particular murder case.

Three weeks ago, in a nearby city, the half-nude body of a twenty-seven-year-old housewife had been found. Her killer had been without pity. In his nineteen years as a cop, Steinberg had never seen a murder this savage.

But he gave Lorraine no details. "I want you to start completely fresh. I don't want something I say to bias the way you might handle this."

Lorraine smiled. She was used to police officers taking this approach. What the detective was really saying was that he wanted Lorraine to prove herself. If she could, through her own methods, reconstruct the outline of the murder as the police had, then the detective would know that her clairvoyant powers were real. Curiously enough, even detectives who regularly use clairvoyants remain skeptical of paranormal powers.

"I'd like to think about it overnight," Lorraine said, looking at Ed.

"Murder cases are very troubling for my wife," Ed said. "Sometimes she gets very depressed."

The detective nodded. "I'd really appreciate it if you could help. I'm afraid our investigation isn't getting anywhere." He shook his head. "If you saw pictures of this young woman— She was very beautiful and very vulnerable." He sighed. "She really didn't deserve this."

"Do you have a card?" Lorraine asked.

The detective reached inside his sport coat

pocket, took out a card, and handed it over. "You'll call in the morning, then?"

Lorraine nodded. "In the morning."

The detective stood up. A large man, he now played anxiously with his hat. He seemed on the verge of saying something but was nervous about it. Finally he said, "I suppose this will sound corny but—I got a very good feeling about you when I walked into the classroom, Lorraine. I really did."

Then he put on his hat and left the lounge.

April 3

"Detective Steinberg?"

"Yes."

"This is Lorraine Warren."

"Good morning."

"I didn't get much sleep last night."

"I'm sorry."

"Ed wasn't exaggerating. Working on murder cases takes a lot out of me."

"It's the same for detectives, Lorraine. Believe me."

"Well, I've thought about it and prayed about it and I guess I can't very well turn you down. I mean, you seem to be genuinely moved by this young woman's death."

"I am."

"Then why don't you tell me where we should meet you?"

"I really appreciate this, Lorraine. I really do."

April 4

During the morning, Lorraine met with members of local and state investigation agencies as well as the sheriff's department. Each sketched for her the broad outlines of a horrible murder case.

Janice Baines was the twenty-seven-year-old mother of a two-year-old and the wife of an enterprising young man who owned a convenience store. His ambition, once he got this one up and running, was to start a chain of such stores.

It was from this store that Janice was abducted on the night of her murder.

Other than this, Lorraine Warren was told nothing else.

Around noon, Detective Steinberg took the Warrens to lunch. Over delicious vegetable burgers and coffee, he showed the Warrens their first glimpse of Janice Baines.

The young woman reminded Ed of one of his favorite movies, *Laura*, a 1940s classic in which the painting of a dead woman comes to have a hypnotic power over the detective investigating her murder.

Janice Baines had been that hauntingly beautiful, a vulnerable, almost frail blond woman with soft blue eyes and a shy but appealing smile. In the photo with her was Jennifer, her daughter.

Thinking of all that had happened to Janice Baines—the terrible and senseless taking of her life—both Lorraine and Ed were overcome with anger and remorse.

"Now I know I want to help," Lorraine said. "I want to find the men who killed her."

"Well, I'm going to take you to the spot where the body was found and see if you can help us."

Soon after the trio left the restaurant.

The murder site was a ragged, muddy piece of property that ran alongside a dirty stretch of river. Rusted and deserted cars stood in deep weeds as rats scurried in and out of their unhinged doors.

Lorraine moved around the murder site, pausing every few moments when she felt an image of something begin to form in her mind. Unfortunately, over the next half hour, nothing of any significance came to Lorraine.

She could see the change in Detective Steinberg. He had gone from willing believer to skeptic. He even began making mild little jokes about psychic abilities.

Lorraine's frustration was twofold. Not only did she, out of understandable human pride, want to prove to the detective that she had genuine psychic powers; she also wanted to get the men who had killed Janice Baines. Lorraine already felt bound to the young woman in some inexplicable but powerful way.

After forty-five minutes in which Lorraine was unable to conjure up a single useful psychic image,

Steinberg suggested they go back to the car. Even on so nice a day, the April wind was not without bite.

On the drive back to town, Detective Steinberg said: "Does this happen often?"

"That I'm not able 'see' anything?" Lorraine said.

"Yes."

"Sometimes it does."

"I'm sorry I made those jokes. I shouldn't have."

"That's all right. I don't blame you for being skeptical."

"You remember what I told you when I came into the classroom—that I had a good feeling about you?"

"Yes."

"Well, I still do, Lorraine."

She smiled. "Thanks. That's a nice thing to hear at a time like this."

"If you turn anything up, let me know."

"I will. I promise."

April 8

Rumbling thunder woke Lorraine. A strobic flash of lightning cast the Warren bedroom into momentary silver relief. Next to her Ed, exhausted from a long day of doing some heavy repair work on the house, slept soundly.

For several minutes Lorraine remained sitting upright in bed. Vague memories of a dream lingered but when she tried to recapture the dream, it faded like smoke. Then, quietly, she left her bed, pulled on a robe, and went down the hall to the study.

Puzzled as to why she was entering the study, Lorraine decided it was best to go along with this mysterious impulse and see where it led.

Five minutes later she sat at a desk, writing furiously with a ball-point pen on sheet after sheet of plain white paper. She wrote without pause, as if an invisible force controlled her hand.

On the night she died, Janice Baines worked in her husband's store, giving her husband a break from his long daytime stint behind the cash register. She often did this when her husband showed signs of depression, which he did whenever he became over-tired or when the bills they owed kept piling up.

On this particular night, Janice saw the usual cross section of customers, underage teenagers who tried to buy beer she refused to sell them, adults who pumped their own gas on the drive and then came in to pay, people who made their dinner in the store's microwave—the frozen chili or hot dogs that were kept in the freezer and sold for a dollar apiece.

Around nine o'clock, three men in a pickup truck pulled in. Janice recognized them immediately as men who often stopped there. On the nights when she was alone, they usually became a little flirtatious—it was obvious all three of them liked to drink—but they never became threatening in any way.

Tonight, however, they were drinking more than usual. They needed shaves, and from passing too close, Janice could also tell they needed baths. They wore faded and ragged denim clothes and smoked endless cigarettes. One of them had the tattoo of a knife on the top of his right hand. The hand looked badly in need of washing.

After paying for a six-pack of Bud, the tallest of the three said, "You ever get scared here?"

"No," said Janice. "Everybody's very nice to me."

He smirked. "Well, a good-lookin' gal like you all alone at night . . ." He shook his head and then winked at his friends. "Well, I sure wouldn't let no gal of mine stand around so other men could look at her. 'Specially if she was as nice-lookin' as you."

All three men laughed and for the first time Janice became aware of how grotesque they were—teeth in need of repair, scars on various parts of their faces, eyes that were always malevolent, even when they were smiling.

One of them reached out to touch her shoulder. She jumped back, screaming.

The men all started laughing and poking each other.

They had succeeded in doing exactly what they'd wanted to do—scaring Janice.

The first man picked up the beer Janice had bagged for him and led the way out of the store. He paused at the door and looked back with a leer. "Maybe we'll see you a little later, babe."

She could tell that the man—despite his filthy

skin and shabby clothes—imagined himself to be quite cool with the ladies. She would have smiled but she did not want to anger him.

The men went out on the drive and drove away, ancient muffler rumbling into the darkness.

Janice's first impulse was to call her husband and tell him what had happened. But no, that would only upset him, and he'd been under too much stress lately, anyway.

The other alternative was to call the police.

She picked up the phone and began dialing.

Then stopped.

No; given the fact that the men had made no overt threat to her, the police could do nothing.

Nothing.

For the next hour and a half, Janice was busy with customers, and eventually she began to put the incident in perspective.

Three crude, drunken men trying to impress each other with their prowess with women.

No big deal.

Happens all the time.

Around eleven-thirty—when her relief was due in fifteen minutes—the three men returned.

By now they were very drunk.

She could see that by the way they stumbled over the threshold and by the frank way they looked at her.

No inhibitions now.

None whatsoever.

She knew enough to dive for the phone but it was already too late.

The tallest of the three went over and ripped the phone from the wall.

The second one put his hand on her breast and squeezed so hard she was forced to cry out.

Frantically, she searched the drive for any sign of a customer.

None.

She was alone with these three men.

The first rape took place in the rear of the store. They knocked her unconscious with fists and then took their turns with her.

After wrapping her body in butcher paper, they set her in back by the door and brought the truck around. They put her inside and then drove away quickly. One of the men knew that her replacement would be there soon.

They took her to the site near the rusted-out cars in the deep weeds.

As they drove, they kept on drinking and fueling drink with marijuana.

Once they reached the site, they laid Janice out on the ground. The tall one took his cigarette and burned her naked breast with it.

Laughing, he knelt down and began burning other parts of her body.

The other two joined in.

Only once did Janice regain consciousness. She could see just enough to start screaming. When she did so, the tall one put his hands on her throat and began choking her.

The other two stood over him, urging him on.

When he was sure she was dead, he pulled down her pants and entered her.

When he was finished with her, the other two took their turns again.

Then they got out of there, leaving Janice's body behind.

"I'm sorry to wake you."

"That's quite all right."

"And apologize to your wife too, Detective Steinberg."

"I will." He laughed softly. "Now what can I do for you at four A.M.?"

She told him about the automatic writing, not in detail, but enough that she could feel him becoming more and more excited on the other end of the phone.

"Do you know what the men look like?"

"Yes," Lorraine said, and told him.

"Do you know what kind of truck they drove?"

"Yes."

"Do you have any idea where we can locate them?"

"That, I don't think so."

"My God, this thing is breaking wide open."

"Yes," Lorraine Warren said, "yes, isn't it."

And then she began crying because she was so happy.

An image of beautiful young Janice filled her mind—now her killers would be caught.

And punished.

The three men Lorraine Warren described to Detective Steinberg were later apprehended, charged, and convicted of murder.

Case File:

BIGFOOT

WE had never paid much attention to stories about Bigfoot. I wouldn't say that we dismissed them as fictitious, but Bigfoot just didn't hold much interest for psychic investigators. That changed one spring when we were lecturing in Tennessee and a reporter from the Elk-Valley Times contacted us and told us about some hill people who kept insisting that something was threatening their children. . . .

—Lorraine Warren

At first, Lorraine dismissed what she seemed to be hearing. This was the end of a long day during which she, Ed, several college students interested in the supernatural, and two hill people had spent many hours tracking through the wild brush of the land surrounding the small encampment where Bigfoot had supposedly been spotted.

None of this had been a pleasant experience for Lorraine. For one thing, the land itself was alien— vast hills and forests so impenetrable they seemed beyond the reach of civilization. For another, Lorraine had never seen poverty this raw within the continental United States.

A handful of shacks perched on the side of sloping hills. The only electricity was a piece of wire that stretched from a pole and snaked along the ground in front of the shacks. At night, the wire lit up like a giant Fourth of July sparkler, casting a dim glow over the huddled shacks. There was no water and thus no plumbing. The outhouses were rank in the hot air.

As for the people, they were dirty, in dire need of dental help and probably complete physical check-ups, and they spoke the halting, inarticulate language of the poorly educated. Lorraine felt great compassion for them and wished there were some way she could improve their lot. And that was what led to her growing depression—there was nothing she could do to help these people. Nothing.

Perhaps it was her guilt that caused her to spend all day with them. Even though she did not necessarily believe their tale of an often-glimpsed ape man that seemed intent on stealing the children of this small settlement, still Lorraine listened courteously while Ed and the students ran a tape recorder and had each settlement person tell his or her version.

One woman's was particularly frightening. She told of how the creature, sneaking from behind a tree, reached out and attempted to touch her two-year-old's hand. The woman had shrieked and run back to the settlement. Alarmed, the men and boys armed themselves with clubs and went into the deep underbrush.

This had happened the day before the Warrens arrived. You could easily see that the people were terrified.

Soon Lorraine found herself in mountainous land dense with ash, beech, and hickory trees and virtually choked with beautiful plants. There roamed black bear and wildcat, white-tailed deer, and foxes. The air was sweet with the song of mockingbird and bluebird and woodpecker. Two poisonous snakes inhabit the area: diamondback and copperhead rattlers. The ragged country is occasionally divided by deep gorges that have not changed since the time Daniel Boone first came here.

This was the land Lorraine encountered when

she and the others went searching that foggy morning.

Most of the day was ill-spent climbing slopes, carefully descending steep hills, flicking chiggers from clothes and body. Only one person irritated her, a rather flip student with a battery-operated bullhorn that he used excessively as a joke. After a break for a sack lunch, Lorraine found herself tired and her mind wandering. A four-day lecture tour was upcoming, and she needed to be fresh for it. After a day such as this one, she was going to be anything but fresh.

Around four-thirty that afternoon, Lorraine first became aware of a disturbing presence in the area. The group had just finished walking through a clearing where the tall grass was mysteriously beaten down, as if something very heavy had rolled over it again and again.

Standing by a tree, taking a break from two solid hours of hiking, Lorraine's mind suddenly offered her a picture of a curious creature. He did, in fact, appear to be a fusion of man and ape, a tall slope-shouldered animal with very long arms that were covered with almost shaggy hair. His face was flat with a protruding bony shelf above the eyes. Two things about him were especially disturbing—first, his eyes, which shone with intelligence, compassion, and fear. Second, his ability to project images telepathically into Lorraine's mind. No so-called dumb animal is able to accomplish such projections.

Lorraine knew instantly that she was dealing here with a creature who—despite his fearsome and ugly appearance—was not the prehistoric beast most people assumed him to be.

The image changed then.

She saw rocky caves above the smashing black water of a furious river. At the edge of the cave stood this creature and, behind him other, similar creatures. The ape man looked out sadly at the vast water. She sensed he was trapped and felt isolated.

Once again the image changed.

This time, she knew, the creature was showing her himself as he was then—just forty or fifty yards away in deep brush and forest.

He was hurt, his hairy, splayed foot scabbed with still-seeping blood. During his travels that day, he had somehow injured his foot. Afraid that his injury would keep him from returning to his secret cave, the creature now projected great fear.

He wanted to see his mate again.

And his children.

But he sensed that the humans with Lorraine would seize him and kill him.

Now they began to communicate mind to mind, Lorraine explaining quickly that he had terrified the small settlement when he had reached out and attempted to touch the human child.

The creature shook his head, saying that he had only been trying to communicate with the child. Youngsters don't have the prejudices of adults, and so he felt he could perhaps explain himself to the child just as he was explaining himself to Lorraine.

Lorraine was determined to go into the brush

and find the creature. But as she moved, others in her party came close to her and began talking.

She asked them for silence, said that she was trying to make herself psychically sensitive to her environment.

She heard her heart loud in her chest.

Felt her hands begin to shake from anxiety.

Being sensitive to the needs of animals ever since she was a young girl—her parents' house a virtual menagerie of dogs, cats, and birds—she felt almost maternal to the creature now.

Sliding away from the others, pushing herself through shoulder-high undergrowth, she began to smell an almost acrid odor and knew this as the creature's scent. Many people who had come near the creature complained of such an odor, and now Lorraine knew why.

She projected images to the creature of her examining his foot, of helping him bind and mend the injury.

His projections were similarly gentle. He showed himself standing on the ledge of a cliff, dawn coming up, with a hawk standing on his wrist. He raised his arm to the rising sun and the hawk glided upward with silky black elegance, a silhouette against the red circle of morning sun.

I am coming to you, Lorraine said to him. *I will help you. I will be your friend*.

For the first time, she sensed the fear easing somewhat in the hairy creature.

He continued to project images of peace and comfort.

Lorraine drew closer, closer.

And then, behind her, the bullhorn sounded.

Immediately the images the creature projected changed. Became violent.

She saw him hurrying through the undergrowth, fleeing back to the cave. But there was pain. Great pain. His foot. Bleeding more than ever now.

And terror.

She—the human creature—was not his friend after all.

And the loud—violently loud—noise of the strange instrument proved it.

The creature covered its ears, the sound of the bullhorn as painful as the injury to its foot.

And fled.

Now Lorraine understood that the creature was once again projecting events as they happened.

She saw him limping up a hill, running as fast as he possibly could. Stumbling, then, regaining his feet; stumbling once more.

His entire body was shaking with fear and exhaustion now. Pain almost blinding.

Hurry.

Flee.

Behind her once more, the bullhorn sounded. Then came the smirking college student calling her name, teasing her, knowing how much she disliked the noise.

No more mind-to-mind images then.

The creature was gone.

Along with his projections.

Stumbling.

Running.

Gone.

Lorraine spent the next twenty minutes trying not to confront in some way the student with the bullhorn. Sensing her great anger, he knew enough to put away his horn and to stay away from Lorraine.

Following the creature's path as best she could—asking the others to let her explore alone in case there was a psychic link-up once again—Lorraine went deep into the brush.

Proof that the creature had been there was easily seen. Blood of a type both redder and more viscous than human blood tainted leaves and grass and foliage.

She followed the blood trail all the way to the edge of a cliff—perhaps the same cliff on which the creature had stood with the hawk on its wrist—and there lost it.

The creature was indeed gone.

Ed: "They are called Tulpas, physical manifestations that are in fact projections of the mind. They are the creatures of black magic as practiced throughout the world but most notably by the monks in Tibet.

"It is my belief that Bigfoot is a Tulpa, a mind projection. So is the Loch Ness monster and many other now-you-see-it-now-you-don't creatures that get reported in the press. Someone who is practicing black magic projects such creatures and we 'see' them. This could also account for unidentified flying objects.

"The most famous Tulpa of recent years was a tiger seen by a United States senator as well as, a bit later, a traffic cop and a bus driver. These men, sober and intelligent, all swore that after seeing the tiger, it just vanished.

"Not until Lorraine's experience with Bigfoot did I realize its true origins. Many other psychic investigators now share my opinion."

Case File:

JANE
SEYMOUR

An Interview with Lorraine Warren

FROM time to time I've met celebrities in the course of an investigation. I've never met a nicer celebrity than Jane Seymour. Jane accompanied me on a case I was investigating in Malibu.

—Lorraine Warren

Q: When you first met Jane Seymour, she was doing what?

Lorraine: I met her at the home of Charles Mases in Beverly Hills. Jane and I went to the studio where Paul Michael Glaser was filming the Houdini film.

Q: This was in Hollywood?

Lorraine: Yes, I was out there to look into several cases. Ed was not there. It was during this time I was tested for my psychic ability at U.C.L.A. by Dr. Thelma Mass. I came out well above average. A mutual friend introduced Jane to me. At the time, Jane was considering some career moves.

Q: You stayed on the set that day?

Lorraine: No, our friend took us to a yogurt restaurant. This was back in the seventies before yogurt bars had come in vogue. I was surprised and pleased. All that delicious food and very little calories. Over lunch, anyway, that's how the subject of the Malibu house came up.

Q: What Malibu house?

Lorraine: Our friend had a friend who owned a house in Malibu. An Episcopal priest was staying there and he was having some problems.

Q: Did they know then what kind of problems?

Lorraine: Not exactly. It seemed that there was a suspicion—though this had never been proven exactly, not even by the police—that a murder had taken place in that house.

Q: Earlier, you mean?

Lorraine: Many, many years earlier. Probably decades.

Q: And the house had changed owners?

Lorraine: Oh, the house had changed owners many times but there were always these whispered stories about "problems," though no one could or would tell us exactly what the problems were.

Q: So the three of you went—you and Jane and your friend?

Lorraine: Yes.

Q: It was a nice place?

Lorraine: It was a spectacular place, set on a cliff above the ocean, a breathtakingly beautiful living room, and a deep blue swimming pool with flowering plants—and beyond that was the ocean. I probably seemed like a star-struck little girl that day—I'd just never seen any place that gorgeous.

Q: Did you get any sense that the house was disturbed in any way?

Lorraine: Yes. Right away, in fact. But it wasn't anything specific. Sometimes when you walk into a place, certain images come to mind, but here . . . well, nothing specific.

Q: How did you spend your time there?

Lorraine: Being entertained by the Episcopal priest who told us how the family who owned the house had "adopted" him while he was on sabbatical and how good they were to him.

Q: Did he show you around the place?

Lorraine: He was a very gracious host and, to be honest, I almost hated to leave there. Until I went up into the master bedroom.

Q: You found something there?

Lorraine: Yes, something that startled me.

Q: Can you describe it?

Lorraine: I can try. I didn't "see" this in the sense

of psychic imaging, but I did have a sense that
there had once lived in this house a man who
had met death under tragic circumstances.
Probably a violent death, though I couldn't be
sure. When I began sensing this, I asked the
others around me not to say anything while I
was trying to communicate with this spirit.
They agreed.

Q: So you did contact him?

Lorraine: Yes, briefly.

Q: But nothing specific came to mind?

Lorraine: Well, after we were finished in one room,
we went into the master bathroom, which was
appointed with gold fixtures and black marble.
Here I got one specific image. I saw a man
with blood on his hands—probably the killer—
washing his hands in the sink. I got frightened.

Q: Did anybody "see" anything?

Lorraine: The priest told me that he frequently had
an image of a dark stranger dressed in white.

Q: Did anything else happen?

Lorraine: Several things. After we got back from
dinner, we sat around the fireplace at this massive table and there I began to communicate
with the dead man. He hadn't wanted to die and
wouldn't accept his death, which was why people in the house became aware of him from time
to time. I think he began to understand the
process he was holding at bay.

Q: So it ended there?

Lorraine: No, as sometimes happens, the after-
math of the whole incident was very strange.

Sometimes things happen to you that don't seem to have any bearing on the case you're investigating but do in some way tie together.

Q: And that happened here?

Lorraine: Oh, yes. The next day, on the plane ride back east, we experienced a kind of air turbulence we'd never known was possible. Literally, the plane was being thrown around. For help, I prayed to a priest friend of mine I knew near home. I asked him to intercede with God and see that our flight would be safe. Then the next day, totally unexpectedly, the priest called me and said that he'd been getting a very strong signal from me yesterday. I told him about the flight and my prayers.

Q: You felt that had bearing on the case?

Lorraine: I feel that sometimes, when you brush up against evidence of the demonic, the dark forces want to warn you away.

Q: And that's what this was?

Lorraine: I believe so, yes.

Q: How about Jane Seymour? Have you kept in touch?

Lorraine: No, though a few years ago I met Jane and her little girl at Heathrow Airport. Her girl is so beautiful I couldn't possibly describe her! At the time, Jane was pregnant with her son Sean and looking radiant. She's really such a classy lady in every respect. We had a nice chat and then went our separate ways.

Case File:

THE EXORCISM AND THE TEENAGE GIRL

WHENEVER we give talks, the one question people usually ask concerns exorcism and the book and film The Exorcist. *They want to know if* The Exorcist *presents a realistic portrait of being possessed by a demon and having that demon driven out through the difficult and often dangerous process of exorcism.*

Our reply is that, yes, in most respects The Exorcist *is a fine and truthful work. Perhaps even more important, both the book and the film helped people understand that there is a spirit realm surrounding us and that*

51

sometimes ordinary lives can be pulled into this realm—and sometimes never escape.

During our world travels, Ed and I met a most splendid priest named Father Michael Elemi. A Nigerian, Father Elemi was spending a few weeks at a college in Nova Scotia when we first saw him. After our talk, he came forward and introduced himself, telling us about the world of the supernatural as it manifested itself in his native Africa.

We knew immediately that we were in the presence of a most gifted man. He spoke fluently of the supernatural and of terrifying incidents in his native land. A small and most dignified man, he possessed the gravity peculiar to people who had done battle with the spirit realm. While he often smiled and laughed, you could see in his dark eyes a somber wisdom that no amount of joviality could quite chase away.

Instantly we became the best of friends, and over the next few years our paths crossed in ways we knew to be fated.

Two years after our first meeting, while Ed and I were completing a book, we learned that Father Elemi was staying for a few months at a Catholic rectory in New Hampshire. No sooner had we called him, happy to plan a long, leisurely weekend together, than we received a disturbing phone call that would unite the three of us in an angry battle with the world of possession and demons.

The case illustrated perfectly a point we make frequently in our lectures: Many people who become possessed bring this situation on themselves.

We spoke for forty-five minutes to a nearly hysterical woman who told us many sad things about her sixteen-year-old daughter. Now, I should say at this point that we receive many phone calls from distraught people. Given our national television appearances, and the extensive coverage our cases have received in the press, we're well known to people who believe they are having problems with demonic infestation, which can result in many things, including possession. Our experience has taught us, however, that many such "infestations" are in fact the result of psychological problems, and as a consequence we often refer the callers to priests, psychiatrists, and social workers.

This woman's call was different. What she outlined was the classic pattern through which a demon is called unwittingly into a home, virtually invited by someone in that home to take over his or her life.

We returned the woman's call, telling her that a priest familiar with the rites of exorcism would be joining us.

The woman, grateful, then confided one piece of information that she had kept from us.

In order to meet and interview her daughter, we would have to travel to downstate New

Hampshire where the girl was presently being · held in a mental institution . . .
                              —Lorraine Warren

Call her Cindy McBain. Fifteen years old. Taffy-colored hair touching slender shoulders. A pretty if slightly melancholy face. A virgin in the strict sense, though she has "experimented" with a few boys in the same way that she "experimented" a few times with marijuana. A good but not spectacular high school student.

Three nights a week and both days of the week-end, Cindy spends time where the rest of her friends do—at the nearby shopping mall. There, she wanders through stores looking at clothes, records, jewelry. Mostly, however, she sits at one of the tables that surround a small shop called "The Hot Dog Hutch," which is where the boys she's interested in also sit.

Time at the Hutch consists of joking, gossiping, and making plans for weekend nights . . . plans that never seem to come true. Usually Cindy spends Saturday night in the company of her girlfriends. Generally this means a movie at the four-plex located across the mall's wide parking lot. None of the boys Cindy likes asks her out, and this has led not only to frustration but to a growing sense that there's something wrong with her. Other girls get dates . . . but not Cindy.

Does her mirror lie? Is she not as attractive as her reflection leads her to believe? A few months before all this begins, a friend of hers says one day:

"Cindy, your problem is that you try too hard. You scare boys away."

Secretly Cindy admits that this is probably true, but every time she gets around a boy she likes she finds herself becoming this shrill, slightly pushy girl she scarcely recognizes—herself.

On a rainy April afternoon, the Saturday shoppers happy to be in the artificial warmth and light of the mall, Cindy finds herself alone. Two friends have the flu, another has gone to visit her brother at college. And if any of the boys who pass in and out of the Hutch are interested in her, they seem to be keeping this fact a secret.

Cindy eats a lunch of a grilled cheese sandwich and a diet Coke (ironically, for all the time she spends at the Hutch, she hates the tart taste of hot dogs) and then, having nothing better to do, begins walking around the mall.

Near the north end of the sprawling shopping complex, there are tiny storefronts that house businesses that appear and die as quickly as fireflies on a hot summer night. These businesses are usually specialty shops—variously, they have included a place that custom-made dolls; a macrame boutique; and a business that allowed you to make your own rock video—and they are doomed in an almost sad way to failure.

By midafternoon Cindy has wandered down to this end of the mall. She notices that one of the tiny storefronts houses a new business, "The Antique Attic."

Cindy goes inside—actually she has no interest

whatsoever in antiques—and begins browsing through the merchandise. Many of the items are tagged with descriptive notes that make no sense to her—"Neo-classic" and "Diamond faceted" and "Doulton stoneware."

The shopkeeper offers Cindy a wan smile but nothing else. Obviously teenagers are not particularly welcome in such a place.

Cindy is about ready to leave when she notices, near the back, above an aged jack-in-the-box, something she's long been curious about: a Ouija board.

Cindy feels the sort of excitement that fills her when a cute boy passes.

She stands on tiptoes and takes the board down and begins to look at it. She has no idea how long she's been standing there, staring at the somewhat battered board with its letters and occult symbols, before the owner comes up behind her.

"May I help you?"

"This board."

"Yes?"

"It's—for sale?"

The woman smiles. "Yes, and very inexpensively."

"Really?"

The woman smiles again. "I took it as part of a big lot of things. Actually, it sort of gives me the creeps. I don't like—you know, supernatural things."

Saturday being allowance day, Cindy has ten dollars in her pocket. "Would you take five dollars for it?"

"I'd be happy to."

Five minutes later, the Ouija board under her arm, Cindy leaves the store, to be caught up in the flow of mall traffic once again. . . .

"I feel something," Nancy said.

"Feel something?" Cindy asked. "Like what?"

"Like—something in this room—some kind of presence or something. Really, Cindy. Really."

Nancy Balkan was a very plump girl with a strikingly appealing face. Now she sat cross-legged on Cindy's bed. For the past three months Cindy had been experimenting with the Ouija board. At first, her experiments were little more than idle fun. She did not believe the board had any powers, magical or otherwise.

But Nancy's sudden fear and the oppressive gray day gave Cindy an involuntary chill. "Nancy, don't you know we're just playing?"

"Listen."

"To what?"

"Shhh. Listen. Hear it?"

"Hear what?"

"Listen."

Much as she didn't want to admit it, Cindy did in fact hear a vague rasping noise. It seemed to be coming from the wall beneath her Michael Jackson poster. From *inside* the wall.

Cindy laughed, telling herself that spooks and

phantoms didn't appear in bedrooms filled with stuffed animals, records and tapes, and a wall filled with snapshots of high-school heartthrobs.

Spooks and phantoms appeared only at night inside shadowy mansions. Right?

But as she sat there, watching her friend Nancy become more and more frightened, Cindy knew that she was in fact hearing something . . .

A noise like that of something scratching to get out . . .

. . . to be set free . . .

Nancy jumped up from the bed and said, "I'm sorry, Cindy. I can't do this anymore."

"Nancy, if you're my friend, you'll stay here with me and see . . . what happens." Cindy's eyes were fixed on the Michael Jackson poster.

Her ears were fixed on the scratching, which was becoming more and more like clawing.

As she rushed to the door and freedom, Nancy said, "You should get rid of that board, Cindy, before it's too late—before something really terrible happens."

Cindy stared down at the board. Square, with chipping paint and lurid occult symbols, the thing resembled something that had been lifted from a trash can. It could have no powers at all. . . .

The clawing—

"You'd better tell your mother what's going on here, Cindy. You'd better tell her right now!"

Nancy slammed the door behind her. Cindy, lying back on the bed, could hear her friend's feet slapping down the stairs.

Then, distantly below, the front door slammed.

Cindy started to close her eyes—to get control of herself and the moment—when the noise inside the wall grew louder.

The clawing—

Cindy's love of food was notorious. Whether it was McDonald's or a pricy restaurant, Cindy would always linger long after the others were through, eating with the appetite of a farmhand at day's end. Fortunately, her metabolism was such that none of her indulgences showed. Slender, quick, she had the sort of figure most girls wanted.

But lately—this was now four months after bringing the Ouija board into her home—friends noticed that Cindy no longer ate much. Her once-splendid figure was now gaunt and her merry blue eyes seemed dulled, as if a light deep within them had ceased glowing.

Friends weren't the only ones concerned about Cindy. Teachers, counselors, and family members tried to find out what was going on with her . . . what could possibly be affecting her life so drastically.

Cindy's mother: "It was about this time that I heard the noises up in her room. Her father, who is a doctor and who likes logical explanations for everything, said that Cindy was merely singing along with her tapes, but I didn't think so.

"There was a disturbing quality to the sound—almost like moaning—and then one day I realized what it was, and I had a most difficult time dealing with it. What I seemed to be hearing were the sounds of people making love.

"At first, I just refused to believe it. We'd raised Cindy in a very proper way, and even if she did occasionally spend some time with a boy, I just knew that she was still a virgin.

"I didn't want to rush up to her room and make a fool of myself. For the next few days, I contented myself with my husband's explanation—that Cindy was just going up to her room and singing along with the tapes she likes to play.

"But one Thursday, the moaning got very loud—so loud that my youngest son began smiling knowingly to himself—so I went up the stairs, knocked on the door and went in.

"By that time I had prepared myself for the worst. I had assumed that Cindy had let a boy into her room—perhaps he'd climbed up the latticework on the back of the house—and that they were making love in Cindy's bed.

"I was astonished to find Cindy on her bed with the headphones on, listening to music. She was all alone.

"She was as startled as I. She took off her headphones and asked why I was there.

"Something in her tone told me that she was no longer the daughter I knew. For the first time, I saw how much weight she'd lost, how dark the circles were under her eyes, how she'd taken to biting her nails until they were bloody.

"Then I saw the Ouija board. Because we have a cleaning woman come in twice a week, I don't often go into Cindy's room. You know how teenagers are about their privacy. I'd never noticed the Ouija board before.

"While my husband was raised Protestant, I was raised a strict Catholic, and even a glance at the Ouija board told me it was a sinister presence. I asked Cindy why she'd have such a thing in her room, and she told me that it was none of my business. Only rarely did she talk back to me in this way.

"I reached over for the board but she slapped my hand away. 'Leave it alone. It's mine,' she said. Her voice wasn't normal. There was a different timbre to it.

"Once again I reached out to take the board from her. This time, instead of slapping my hand away, she grabbed my arm. Her grasp was incredibly strong and hurt me a great deal. For the first time in my life, I was afraid of my daughter.

"Tears in my eyes, I left her room, with Cindy behind me clutching her board protectively, cuddling it the way you would an infant.

"She stayed in her room until her father got home. When I told him what had happened, he immediately went upstairs. He got the same response from Cindy. She seemed upset and angry and she wouldn't let him so much as touch the Ouija board.

"When he came downstairs, his face was a chalky white and he had nothing to say. He went into the den and sat there in the darkness for half an hour. I'd never seen him so . . . defeated. There's no other way to describe it. I've never been sure what happened up there, but something took away my husband's self-confidence. He seemed broken by the experience."

The next three weeks in the McBain home became the sort of nightmare Cindy's mother would otherwise have considered common only on cheap TV movies.

The clawing in the walls became so pronounced that it could be heard throughout the house.

The sound of sexual ecstasy emanating from Cindy's room could now be heard as far away as the formal dining room.

Cindy herself became a virtual stranger given to sudden rages and inconsolable sobbing. A minister, a priest, and a psychiatrist were consulted. None were able to help. Cindy quit school, quit eating all but for sustenance, and would not directly address any member of her family.

Her father, desperate, broke into her room in an attempt to steal the Ouija board and destroy it.

He had taken no more than two or three steps across the threshold before Cindy flung herself at him, slapping him viciously, slamming his head into the wall again and again.

Though a grown man, and a strong one, Dr. McBain was forced to use all his strength to push his daughter away.

A quick search of the room—while Cindy hurled a variety of objects at him—revealed nothing. Cindy had obviously hidden the Ouija board.

In two more weeks, after three sessions with a psychiatrist, Cindy McBain was taken to a psychiatric hospital upstate. It was at this time that her mother contacted the Warrens.

Mrs. McBain said, "Even though she'd been hospitalized and given several different kinds of tranquilizers, Cindy had not calmed down to any appreciable degree. She still flew into rages and she still consulted her Ouija board . . . that was the most perplexing thing of all. Somehow, Cindy had managed to sneak the Ouija board into the hospital. We have no idea how she did this . . . but late one night an attendant came into her room and saw her there in the moonlight on her bed, the Ouija board in front of her."

On an overcast spring day, Lorraine and Ed Warren drove to the rectory to pick up Father Elemi. The trio drove first to the McBain home, where Mrs. McBain showed them Cindy's room and revealed two key points she had not discussed on the phone.

Ed says, "The first thing she told us was that Cindy's experimentation had gone much farther than just the Ouija board. She and her friends had been buying paperbacks on the occult and trying out many of the oaths and rituals they'd found in the books. Cindy had been much more deeply immersed in the supernatural than her mother had led us to believe.

"The second thing Mrs. McBain told us was that she herself had seen a black shape moving down the upstairs hallway one day. The shape seemed to be composed of black fog. It had gone into Cindy's room. Mrs. McBain had been afraid to tell any-body—including us—about the shape because she assumed that we would think she was losing her mind.

"Any doubts we'd had about demonic infestation and possession were gone now. This was a classic case of somebody experimenting with the occult and virtually—if not literally—inviting the demon into the household.

"We told Mrs. McBain that we should reach Cindy as soon as possible. She phoned ahead to the hospital and told the doctor in charge what we intended to do. While he was reluctant to cooperate at first, he did finally agree that none of his attempts to help Cindy had worked.

"Mrs. McBain pressed the matter, and the doctor told us to come ahead. She then phoned her husband at his office. He said he would meet us in two hours at the hospital where Cindy was a patient."

The hospital was a brooding shape of brick set against a deep forest. Iron gates stopped you at the main entrance. An armed guard in a rain poncho appeared, ascertained their business, and then let the car pass.

Inside, the hospital walls were painted in restful earth tones. Nurses in starched white uniforms moved about efficiently. Dr. Gertner greeted the group on the third floor and after some consultation took the Warrens, Father Elemi, and Mrs. McBain to Cindy's room.

Dr. McBain was already there. He sat solemnly on the edge of his daughter's bed in the small, clean room. Cindy, wearing a pair of blue silk pajamas, her hair caught back in a soft chignon, paid no attention whatsoever to him. Her eyes were dulled to an unseeing madness, as if she were responsive only to voices within, the same way some schizophrenics behave.

Dr. McBain greeted the arrivals sadly and then let them proceed.

Before going to the McBain home, Father Elemi and the Warrens had discussed their plans, which the priest now carried out.

As he quietly approached the girl, uttering soft and reassuring words, Father Elemi took from inside his black garb a small crucifix.

Cindy began screaming.

The priest had not even rested the crucifix against Cindy's knee before she jerked back into the corner of her bed and began cursing the small man foully.

Shocked, her parents began pleading with her to behave. The Warrens calmed them down and said that all this was a necessary part of the plan.

Cindy's eyes changed from blue to a deep amber color and silver spittle foamed at the corners of her mouth.

Father Elemi began speaking not to the girl, but to the demon inside her.

"You will be banished," he said.

Cindy reached up and tried to slap the crucifix from the priest's hand.

Dr. McBain led his sobbing wife from the room.

The Warrens and Father Elemi stood over Cindy. "We're here to help you," Lorraine said gently. "And we can help you."

The demon made a throaty, threatening noise inside Cindy's chest.

Father Elemi, knowing exactly what was going on, withdrew the crucifix.

Ed said, "We'll be back soon, Cindy. Very soon."

The next eighteen hours were rushed. Father Elemi had to obtain permission from the rectory where he was staying to perform an exorcism. He also requested another priest to assist him with the ritual. After much discussion, the chancellor agreed to Father Elemi's request.

"We'd always known that Father Elemi was special, even for a priest. But to see him fast and meditate in preparation for the exorcism was one of the most moving experiences in our lives," Lorraine said.

"It's called a 'Black Fast,'" Ed added. "All the priest eats are small amounts of bread and water. Father Elemi spent most of his time alone, praying. He walked a great deal, and we started to worry about his physical endurance. We wondered if such a small man could stand up to all this—especially the exorcism itself, which is one of the most physically demanding rites in the church."

For an exorcism, the priest wears a purple stole symbolizing penance and humility. The priest begs God through prayers to free the possessed person of the demon. One part of the ceremony consists of adjurations to the devil, demanding that Satan, in the name of Christ, the Blessed Virgin, and all the saints, leave the person or home immediately. In some cases the ritual consists of the priest demanding that the spirit or spirits speak out and identify themselves.

Finally, there are the instruments the priest uses: holy water, a crucifix, and a relic of a saint, which are all applied to the body in the same fashion—touched to the head or breast, for example—in the course of the exorcism.

Despite popular misconceptions, there is no chanting during the ritual. The priest prays in a loud, strong voice, many times in Latin. The priest assisting him sees that certain candles stay lit and that cruets for water and wine, a missal, small hand bells, and a gold chalice are at hand. He becomes, in effect, an altar boy.

This was the scene in Cindy's hospital room two

days later as a cold, harsh rain fell outside and as a nervous psychiatrist paced the hall wondering if he was doing the right thing by letting this ritual go forward.

By now Father Elemi was showing the effects of the Black Fast. His hands twitched, his eyes seemed glassy from lack of sleep, and his voice was little more than a rasp.

The exorcism began.

Lorraine says, "What most people don't realize is how violent such a ceremony can become. The demon has possessed a body and soul and does not want to let go. Cindy looked as if she were being shot with invisible bullets. She writhed on the bed. Sometimes her screams sounded like sexual ecstasy, sometimes her screams were pure pain.

"But Father Elemi was not turned back. He spoke to the demon and the demon responded in an angry voice. Father Elemi continued the ritual. Loud thumping sounds came from inside the wall. A fetid odor filled the room. You had to cover your mouth and nose. The young priest who was assisting looked very frightened, but it's a credit to his courage that he kept right on going, doing what he was supposed to do, and never leaving Father Elemi's side.

"Cindy hurled objects at the wall, screamed obscenities, moved around on the bed as if taking some kind of sexual pleasure, and finally—as the demon's voice was beginning to fade inside her—lay still on the bed. Sometimes you worry that the person may have died from all the strain.

"The entire ritual took the better part of an hour and when it was completed, Father Elemi's knees began to buckle. He had to be supported. You can't be sure, at first, if the exorcism has been successful.

"The priests packed all their instruments and went out into the hall with the rest of us to wait.

"After half an hour, the McBains went in to see their daughter."

"When we entered the room, Cindy opened her eyes and I felt the first real hope I'd known in months," Dr. McBain said. "Her eyes were back to normal and there was even a small smile on her face."

"I hadn't noticed just how distorted Cindy's voice had become during all this until I walked into her room after the exorcism. She'd always had a soft, pleasant voice but the demon had made it harsh, very unfeminine. Now she sounded like our daughter again," added Mrs. McBain.

Four days later Cindy went home.

Once there, she showed again how loving a daughter she could be. She insisted on straightening her room, helping her mother with dinner, and being pleasant to her younger brother.

Father Elemi, drained completely of his former zest, went into a withdrawal period common to priests who have performed an exorcism. Gradually, over the course of the next five days, he began to regain his strength.

Lorraine, recalling this period, smiles. "His favorite dessert was ice cream, of which we gave him plenty during his recovery. I remember the very first time we offered him ice cream. He put a small spoonful of it on his tongue and let it melt. His entire face lit up with pleasure. It was childlike, a beautiful memory for us."

"Unfortunately, this particular case did not have a happy ending for any of the participants," Ed said. "Three weeks after going back home, the demon reappeared—or had just been lying dormant—inside Cindy. She was taken back to the hospital where doctors debated the best way to treat her. Some scoffed at the whole notion of demons and exorcism. Others weren't so sure. Cindy, now a young woman, leads a somewhat normal life—but she is always subject to what her doctor calls 'attacks.' He calls it mental illness. But we know better.

"As for our good friend Father Elemi, he returned to native Nigeria, which was, at the time, in the throes of civil war. The revolutionary government there hates the Catholic Church and was known to execute priests and nuns.

"Right after his return, Father Elemi was seen by some other priests, but he soon disappeared. He has never been seen again. It's assumed that he was murdered."

Case File:

KILLER
IN THE
MIST

TWENTY years ago law enforcement officers almost never came to our lectures, and those who did were clearly embarrassed about being there. In those days people with psychic gifts—such as mine—were still considered to be at best actors and at worst charlatans.

These days all that has changed.

These days many police departments around the country call regularly on "gifted" people for help in investigations of all kinds.

In my own case, law enforcement officers have put me to work helping find missing *children, helping decide which employees were shoplifting, and helping track down killers.*

One of the strangest cases involved a murder that had gone unsolved for many long months outside a midwestern city . . . a murder that most people assumed would go unsolved forever.

—Lorraine Warren

Maybe if he hadn't known her family, Lieutenant Walter Gresak wouldn't have gotten so entangled in the Wendy Lynott murder case. But now—six months after the slaying—the Lynott case still affected him; it had started to influence his relationship with his wife and two children.

A proud man who had come from the city's worst neighborhood, thirty-eight-year-old Lieutenant Gresak wanted to make certain that working-class people—in this case the parents of Wendy Lynott—got the same first-rate police work enjoyed by the city's more prosperous citizens. For this reason, Gresak became obsessed with what he was doing—a dangerous sign for a police officer investigating something as serious as a murder.

The facts were these: On the night of April 12, twenty-five-year-old Wendy Lynott had been walking home from her job as a check-out clerk at a nearby Target store. As the temperature was mild, well into the sixties, the young woman had apparently taken her time walking along a moonlit gravel path that paralleled railroad tracks.

A switchman in the nearby yards said he saw

Wendy on the path approximately an hour before the time the coroner fixed as her time of death. At this time, the switchman testified, she was alone and looked perfectly safe, enjoying herself on a lovely spring evening.

In the morning her body was found stuffed half in and half out of a concrete culvert a half mile from where the switchman had seen her.

Gresak, who had been assigned the case, was shocked when he learned the woman's identity. He spent most of the investigation's first morning in the drab, modest home of Wendy Lynott's parents, talking to them about her habits, her personal life, and any new people who might have come into her life in recent weeks. After making a list of her friends, Gresak got to work.

As most police officers will tell you, the first twenty-four hours in a murder investigation are critical. With each passing day, the likelihood of catching the killer lessens. Evidence can be destroyed, the killer can leave town, or an alibi can be arranged.

Also, Gresak glumly discovered, the crime scene yielded very little. Male footprints were found near the culvert, but an early-morning rain had washed most of the prints away. Two cigarette butts of a common brand were also uncovered in the weeds, but ultimately they revealed nothing.

To complicate matters, there was even a false confession. A pudgy man in a cheap dark suit strolled into the precinct forty-eight hours later, asked to see Lieutenant Gresak, and promptly told the astounded policeman that he had killed Wendy Lynott because she had been unfaithful to him. The man insisted that he and Wendy had been lovers.

Leery of the man, Gresak ran a background check on him and soon learned that the man had a history of severe mental problems and had twice confessed to murders in the Buffalo area. The man was put in touch with mental health officials and let go.

During the next two weeks, Gresak interviewed every girlfriend, previous boyfriend, and coworker of Wendy's he could find. This was what he learned: While not a pretty girl, Wendy Lynott had been pleasant, outgoing, clever, and eager to be liked. Perhaps too eager. Several friends told Gresak of rather embarrassing relationships the young woman had found herself in.

These affairs all seemed to run the same way— she would begin going out with a man, fall desperately in love with him, and then endure any sort of degradation in order to keep the relationship intact. Friends remarked sadly that she always seemed to choose men who had no respect for her. She'd had a number of opportunities to go out with respectable, and respectful, men, but apparently she was bored with them and invariably found a reason to turn them down.

One of her boyfriends had been particularly vicious, a bodybuilder who ran a local health club. Friends of the dead woman told Gresak that the man—Vic Ready—had on several occasions struck

Wendy, once severely enough that she had to go to a hospital emergency room.

Gresak sensed that Vic Ready might well be the man he was looking for. Unfortunately, after an hour of interviewing the arrogant, uncooperative man, Gresak discovered that the health club manager had an alibi for the night—he was in New York City attending a fitness clinic and spent the night in question surrounded by witnesses.

This is the way most murder investigations go once the early phase is over—following down lead after lead that promises much but delivers little.

Three months passed. It was then that Gresak's coworkers and family began to notice how obsessed he was with the case. He either called or visited the Lynotts weekly, and always with an abiding air of apology and failure, as if repentant for letting them down. He also reinterviewed key people in the investigation every week, hoping they would either change their stories or remember something that would prove helpful.

Hot summer came. Gresak ruined a family vacation by spending most of his time in his motel room placing long-distance calls back to the city, checking and rechecking leads and talking with the Lynotts.

In the final week of summer, Gresak was told by his wife and his commanding officer that the time had come to set the case aside, put it in the OPEN file, and get back to working with equal diligence on other cases. His commanding officer cited the workload strapping his other men, a workload Gresak did not share because he was always working on the Lynott matter. His wife cited the children—they had become afraid of their father. He was now given to bursts of temper and seemed disinterested in family matters. He spent most of his time on the phone.

After a few visits with the psychotherapist who worked with city police officers, Gresak was able to see that the Lynott case had in fact assumed some kind of unhealthy significance for him. He commiserated once more with the Lynotts—who themselves had done a much better job than Gresak about going on with life—and then gave himself to the workaday world of police officers.

That fall he worked on several important and fascinating cases, including the murder of a wealthy dowager that got both Gresak and his partner a lot of TV time. He became a minor celebrity. This helped push the Lynott case from his mind.

Snow flew. Gresak, promoted due to the quick and efficient way he'd handled the dowager's murder, sensed the Lynott case at last beginning to fade. Occasionally a new lead would develop, but a phone call or two proved it to be another dead end. He contacted the Lynotts infrequently and then only over the phone.

During this time, Gresak became caught up in old habits once more, such as sitting in the TV room with the kids and watching sitcoms and cop shows. He found the latter funnier than the sitcoms because TV cop shows always got everything wrong about real-life cops.

One night on TV, however, he saw a show that

disturbed him. An interview show featured as guests Lorraine and Ed Warren, "demonologists" as the host called them. At first, Gresak's skepticism kept him from doing much more than smiling at the couple. He had been raised to believe that anything to do with "psychic investigation" was nothing more than a contrivance, usually aimed at separating somebody from his money.

But as he watched, Gresak found some of his cynicism waning. These were not zealots or wild-eyed satanists. These were appealing, ordinary people who made no special claims for themselves. They weren't silly and they weren't boastful and they weren't invoking any dark powers. They went about their job in a sensible way that grew out of their deep religious faith and the knowledge that many people unwittingly found themselves with problems that involved the supernatural.

The point that most fascinated Gresak, however, was Lorraine's admission that she had many times worked with police departments in trying to find lost people and even in solving murders.

Despite his best intentions, Gresak found himself thinking about the Lynott case again.

What if he asked a woman with psychic gifts to reconstruct the murder and—

Sitting there in the flickering darkness, knowing he should not even pursue this line of thought, Gresak found himself caught up with a new enthusiasm for the Lynott case.

Here, at last, might be a way to—

"Lorraine Warren please."

"This is she."

"My name is Lieutenant Walter Gresak. I'm a police detective. I saw you on TV last night. Since you're in this state, I, uh, wondered if we could talk."

"Sure. On the phone, you mean?"

"For right now, yes."

"Of course."

So Gresak told her about the Lynott case. He was impressed with her response. Again, rather than make extravagant claims, Lorraine Warren told him how fragile her ability to "see" was. Sometimes it worked and was most helpful to authorities; sometimes it produced nothing at all and proved to be a waste of time. Her modesty and her honesty convinced Gresak that she was not a charlatan looking for publicity.

"Is there any way you could come down next Tuesday afternoon?" Gresak asked.

Lorraine consulted her schedule. "Yes."

Gresak gave her the directions to the precinct. Excited, he hung up.

He kept the Warrens' impending visit to himself. He did not want to make either his wife or his commanding officer nervous.

That night Lorraine Warren had trouble sleeping. Before midnight she rose three times, only to stand by the window and gaze out at the dark winter landscape made silver by the moonlight.

An image of a black man's face kept appearing before her eyes, but she was not sure why. She had no idea who the man was. In his thirties, his handsome face suggested both education and intelligence.

But who was he? Why did his image keep imposing itself on her consciousness?

Her last attempt at sleep was fitful indeed. One of the Warrens' cats crawled into bed to sleep beside her, but like her mistress, the cat couldn't sleep either. Finally they both drifted off into an uneasy slumber.

Lorraine came awake with the sounds of a young woman's screams in her mind.

She thought of what Lieutenant Gresak had told her about the murder.

Was Lorraine hearing Wendy Lynott's screams?

And—again—who was the black man?

The drive from the motel took six hours. Heavy wind made the interstate slow going, cars and trucks being whipped around in its fury.

The Warrens reached the precinct half an hour late.

Lieutenant Gresak was a tall, chunky man with graying hair and the air of a former football player gone slightly to seed. On meeting them, he seemed both nervous and slightly embarrassed. The Warrens were accustomed to such greetings. Even people who desperately needed their help had reservations about their true abilities. The Warrens say that, given all the prejudice against supernatural and occult phenomena in our society, this is to be expected.

"Why don't we go?" Lieutenant Gresak said, hurrying them out of the station house, eyes glancing about anxiously. He might have been afraid that somebody would recognize the Warrens from their TV appearance the other night.

As they drove down a rutted gravel road and rode deeper into a rusted-out, ugly section of deserted warehouses and ill-kept railroad yards, Lorraine began to develop a headache.

Forced now to close her eyes every few minutes, the image of the black man began returning. As did the shrill screams of the young woman.

Lieutenant Gresak stopped the squad car on a clay cliff overlooking a deeply forested area below. This was the sort of place, adjacent to a railroad yard, that hobos would use to make small encampments.

When Lorraine was two steps out of the car, the screaming grew louder in her mind. Ed, looking disturbed, took her hand.

Lieutenant Gresak led them down an angling path that stopped at an open area littered with beer cans, cigarette butts, and the fading wrappers of fast-food places. A burned-out fire in the center of the area told them that hobos did indeed use this spot as a gathering place.

As the young woman's screams began to lessen in Lorraine's mind, Wendy's image became vivid.

"Excuse me, Lieutenant."

"Yes?"

"Wendy. Did she have red hair?"

"Yes."

"And green eyes?"

"Yes."

"And a beauty mark to the left of her mouth?"

"Why, yes," Lieutenant Gresak said. "Say, you're—"

"Why don't we just go on," Lorraine said.

Ed and Lorraine followed Lieutenant Gresak away from the cleared area and along a narrow path that wound among the white birches and hardwoods. Wind was trapped in the naked branches and the noise was like that of cracking whips. The grim gray sky only made the day more unpleasant.

Ten minutes down the path, Lorraine heard herself whimpering. The sound came from deep within her chest, and she knew immediately what she was hearing. The images in her mind now showed Wendy Lynott stopping to talk to three men in a car on the night of the murder. Lorraine tried to warn Wendy away from the car.

But Wendy stopped and joked with the men. She seemed to know them. Then one of the men pushed his face into the night air. He was angry. Lorraine saw that he was the same handsome black man that had been in her dream.

"Lorraine, Lorraine, are you all right?" Ed asked, slipping his arm around his wife.

"We're very near."

"Near what, Lorraine?" Lieutenant Gresak asked. It was easy to tell he was excited.

"Near where they killed her."

"The culvert, you mean?"

The body was found in a concrete culvert that jutted out from the side of the hill to their right.

"No," Lorraine said. An image of a white birch tree filled her mind. It was night—and she saw Wendy Lynott pushed roughly against the tree by the black man and . . . two white men.

"There were three of them," Lorraine said.

"Three killers?"

"No; only one did the actual killing. There were two others in addition. White men."

Opening her eyes, Lorraine left the path and walked through deep and tangled bramble, around a huge granite boulder, and then stood facing a white birch tree—

—the same one she had seen moments ago.

Her entire body trembled now. Wendy Lynott's screams once more filled her ears.

"No!" Wendy cried. "No!"

The handsome black man moved toward her. He spoke in a deep, clear voice. There had been a business dealing—drugs, from what Lorraine could tell—and Wendy had betrayed him to a rival. And the man knew it.

He brought his hand down hard against the side of her head.

Wendy cried out once more.

But it was too late. The judo chop sent her into unconsciousness, and then, in a frenzy, the man began to beat her.

When he was sure she was dead, he carried her over to the culvert and shoved her inside.

Tears were warm in Lorraine's eyes as she saw water rush over Wendy Lynott, saw Wendy's frail white legs sticking out of the culvert.

"Honey, what is it?" Ed said cautiously.

She looked at Lieutenant Gresak and smiled. "Would you like a description of the three men?"

Gresak looked five years younger. "You can really do that?"

She nodded.

"Right now?"

"Do you have a notebook?"

Gresak laughed. "You bet I do, Lorraine. You bet I do."

"Three days later, the men in Lorraine's dream were apprehended. For Lorraine, headaches came, hard, debilitating ones. She wasn't sure why," Ed says.

"Sometimes, when she tried to sleep, she could hear Wendy Lynott screaming for help.

"To this day, Lorraine dislikes discussing this particular case. Never before—or since—had her 'sight' been so clear. Never before had her 'visions' cost her so much physically. She suffered from fatigue and anxiety for several weeks afterward."

Case File:

THE DEVIL IN CONNECTICUT

An Interview with Ed Warren

THE case of The Devil in Connecticut dominated worldwide headlines for several months. During that time Lorraine and Ed Warren played an integral part in the unfolding drama. NBC made a television movie entitled The Demon Murders, which documented the role the Warrens played in this disturbing and unforgettable case. Now, looking back several years, Ed Warren reflects on the case and what it came to mean to Lorraine and him.

Q: How did you get involved in the case?

Ed: Very simply. Lorraine and I were sitting at home one Sunday evening and the phone rang. We were told that an eleven-year-old boy was suffering a demonic attack.

Q: Did you go right to the scene?

Ed: No. Over the years, we've learned that many so-called supernatural events are really just people suffering breakdowns of various sorts. They hallucinate, they hear things, and people around them begin to think that they're seeing something from another realm.

Q: You sound skeptical.

Ed: No, not at all. Just sensible. Reasonable. There are so many investigations we *can't* get to—sound, valid ones—that we can't afford to waste our time on illegitimate ones.

Q: But you did eventually get involved with the Glatzel family.

Ed: Oh, yes. We got to know them very well. They became friends.

Q: What did you see when you checked out eleven-year-old David Glatzel?

Ed: Well, we ended up going over there the same night we got the first call. An MD accompanied us. You see, there was sort of a wild card with David Glatzel. He suffered from a learning disability. We knew this physician whose son suffered from the same problem, so we asked him to go along and interpret what he saw. We didn't want to confuse something that stemmed from being learning disabled with something that stemmed from the supernatural. That's why we take doctors and psychotherapists and priests and police officers along whenever possible. This way we ensure that we're getting the situation evaluated from at least two very different perspectives.

Q: Did you know right away that something was wrong with the boy?

Ed: Not with the boy but with the environment.

Q: The environment?

Ed: When I started up the front steps, I tripped. I'm not a particularly clumsy man, but I did a great big pratfall. I hadn't stubbed my foot against the step, I hadn't loosened my grip on the banister—but there I was tripping. It was as if an invisible hand had grabbed my ankle. I went right down, and it so happened that the doctor found this funny. We were close friends and so I knew he was laughing out of affection and not malice. But when I explained to him that I really hadn't tripped, he went, "Sure, sure," and made a joke about how clumsy I was. Then he came right behind me and stumbled too.

Q: Really?

Ed: Absolutely. And you should have seen his expression.

Q: Scared?

Ed: "Scared" would be going too far, but he was certainly disturbed by it.

Q: So then you went inside and examined the boy?

Ed: Yes. The doctor looked him over and found nothing physically wrong with him. Later, we learned more about the effects of his learning disability.

Q: Did it turn out to be an exciting night?

Ed: Very exciting—*too* exciting. The Glatzel family and three of us ended up sitting around the kitchen table later on discussing the problems David was having. They discussed what had set off the latest round of manifestations.

Q: And what was it?

Ed: Earlier in the day, David had been at another house where his parents were visiting. He got tired and laid down. While he was in bed, an old man appeared to him. The old man was dressed in a plaid shirt and jeans with a rip in the right knee and he looked right at David and said "Beware." Naturally, David was terrified. He ran out and told his mother what just happened, but she dismissed it. She thought, naturally enough I suppose, that the boy had just had a nightmare. Well, she took him home and David laid down in his own bed and this time, the same thing happened. There's this old man. He's dressed the same way. His voice is the same timbre. He even says "Beware" again. There's only one thing different with him.

Q: Which is?

Ed: Which is that this time the old man's body looks charred. And one more thing—instead of feet, this time the old man has hooves. Both these factors—the charred body, the cloven feet—are classical symbols of demonic infestation. The old man once more whispered the word "Beware!" Fortunately, by now the mother was starting to take her son seriously.

Q: So she called you?

Ed: No, first she called a priest, an elderly man Lorraine and I have known for many years.

Q: He offered to help Mrs. Glatzel?

Ed: No, he told them to call us. And after we first spoke to Mrs. Glatzel, we called the priest because he knew the family.

Q: Did he think they were exaggerating?

Ed: On the contrary, he was completely convinced they were all telling the truth and that David was indeed suffering a demonic attack.

Q: Did he offer to help you?

Ed: He was afraid. I know that sounds bad, but remember, priests are human too. He's an elderly gentleman and he'd been planning for years to take his mother to Ireland. They were to leave three days later.

Q: Couldn't he at least have come over to the Glatzel house that night?

Ed: Now we're back to his fear. This is a priest who has been involved in many supernatural predicaments before, and they've cost him a great deal.

Q: How so?

Ed: His health isn't very good. He was a healthy man until he started getting involved in certain cases.

Q: He's worked with you?

Ed: Yes.

Q: And it's taken its toll?

Ed: It takes its toll on everybody. Nobody escapes. I've seen my wife, for example, be so crushed by the pressure she was under . . . well, I wondered if she was going to make it.

Q: And that's what had happened to the priest?

Ed: Exactly. He gave us his blessing and said that he would keep us in his prayers constantly . . . but that he was going to Ireland. And I didn't blame him at all.

Q: So you sat in the kitchen at the Glatzel house and what happened?

Ed: It was a terrible night, really frightening. I'll tell you—anybody who doesn't believe in supernatural phenomena should have been there. All their doubts would have been taken care of in thirty seconds. I'd never heard pounding like that.

Q: Pounding?

Ed: When there is the potential of demonic infestation, pounding is frequently heard.

Q: Hammering, you mean?

Ed: Hammering times a hundred. My wife always says it sounds as if somebody is inside the wall and beneath the floor with two-by-fours.

Q: The pounding went on a long time?

Ed: Approximately an hour. And it confirmed what both Lorraine and I were beginning to sense. That David Glatzel was possessed demonically. In fact, it was one of the worst examples of possession we'd ever seen.

Q: Where did the case go from there?

Ed: Well, we spent several months working with six Roman Catholic priests, three of whom were trained in Rome.

Q: David Glatzel got worse?

Ed: Much worse. He suffered what appeared to be periodic breakdowns but which were really infestations. He saw things that frightened him—spirits and demons—and wouldn't leave his room, and he would speak in voices not his own. This confused the family, of course. They didn't know what to do.

Q: Was any of your work effective?

Ed: It helped ease the worst of it but we were dealing with a number of different demons, and they were virtually in complete control of David. They had in effect taken him over and were telling him what to do.

Q: When did the murder take place?

Ed: About a year after we were called into the case, I think.

Q: And it involved whom?

Ed: A young man named Arnie who was engaged to David's sister Debbie. But before I go any further, I should tell you some things about Arnie.

Q: Do your feelings about him jibe with press reports?

Ed: Not the negative ones. Before the murder took place, we got to know Arnie very well. To him, David was like a little brother. Arnie was very, very protective. Really paternal. Arnie helped us with our investigation, was deeply involved with it, as a matter of fact.

Q: So he knew about David's possession all along?

Ed: Oh, yes, and again, whenever Lorraine and I needed something—or one of the priests needed something done—there was Arnie. Sometimes he'd stay up late at night with David, if the boy was having a bad time of it.

Q: This is a very different portrait of Arnie than some newspapers offered.

Ed: The reporters didn't know Arnie. We did. He was a very all-American young man—no smoking, no drinking, certainly no drugs—and he was very respectful of people. *Very* respectful. And I'm not convinced that David could have made it without Arnie. David cared for his family very much, but Arnie was special to him—sort of a role model, I suppose.

Q: The murder took place when?

Ed: Well, it's my opinion that the murder was preordained several nights before it actually happened.

Q: Would you explain that?

Ed: David had been having an exceptionally bad time of it. The demons were trying to take him over totally. Arnie saw what was going on and tried to stop it.

Q: How could he hope to succeed where you had failed?

Ed: He offered himself to the demons.

Q: He did this literally?

Ed: Literally. He'd stand next to David's bed and

hold David's hand and shout at the demons to come and possess him and leave David alone.

Q: And what happened?

Ed: Any time you invite demons into your life, they're inclined to take you at your word.

Q: They possessed Arnie?

Ed: Within the next twenty-four hours, yes.

Q: And then what happened?

Ed: Well, a few afternoons later, Arnie was at work, talking with his boss, and he went insane.

Q: It is my understanding that Arnie and his boss were good friends.

Ed: The best of friends. That's why nobody could believe this when it happened. They were very close.

Q: And Arnie took a knife and—

Ed: —and began stabbing the other man till he was dead.

Q: The trial was one of the most sensational in history.

Ed: It was a circus.

Q: I understand you thought you could have cleared him.

Ed: I didn't have any doubt about that. The tack the prosecuting attorney took, of course, was that here was this mad dog who had to be put away for the sake of society. He didn't seriously consider anything we tried to tell him.

Q: What did you try to tell him?

Ed: The same thing we tried to tell the judge. That what we were dealing with here was a special circumstance. We asked if we could introduce videotapes and audio tapes and eyewitnesses to the trial that would have confirmed our point . . . that Arnie was possessed during the time he killed his boss.

Q: They wouldn't let you?

Ed: They had this superior attitude. They looked at us as if we were charlatans or lunatics.

Q: The world press covered the trial.

Ed: As I said, it was a circus. To be fair to the press—which is often criticized unduly, I think—many of the reporters took us much more seriously than the judge or the prosecuting attorney did.

Q: Arnie was convicted?

Ed: Convicted and sentenced to prison where he served four or five years. He married Debbie—David's sister—while he was in prison, and today they live in this area and have a successful small business and are very decent people.

Q: You see them, then?

Ed: Oh, yes.

Q: And Arnie is free of his demons?

Ed: Yes.

Q: How about David?

Ed: I'm not sure. Nobody is sure.

Q: You've seen him, then?

Ed: Occasionally. As with many such cases, the publicity was traumatic for the family. It was really an ordeal. You're held up to a certain amount of scorn and you feel yourself becoming a different person. Distrustful. Apprehensive when you're around strangers.

Q: Then nobody really escapes possession completely?

Ed: Oh, no. (*Sighs*) It changes your life in ways most people just can't imagine.

Case File:

DEMONIC INFESTATION

An Interview with the Warrens

IN late October 1973 a married couple named Jack and Janet Smurl purchased one half of a duplex in West Pittson, Pennsylvania. On the other side of the duplex lived Jack's parents.

From this innocent beginning came a story that was to create headlines worldwide. Virtually every major news organization in the United States dispatched reporters to find out exactly what was going on in the duplex.

By the time the story ended—though it has yet to "end" in any real sense—the Catholic *church, police organizations, and dozens of neighbors would be drawn into the controversy.*

Lorraine and I found our own lives becoming dominated by the events in the duplex and, like the Smurls themselves, we found ourselves wondering if we would survive the incidents which took place there.

Never before had our abilities to deal with the supernatural been tested to this degree.

—Ed Warren

Q: Did you know right away that you were dealing with an extraordinary event?

Lorraine: Oh, yes. On the first day we drove to West Pittson our van was thrown around on the highway by gusts of wind that nearly caused us to pull over. We took a registered nurse named Rosemary Frueh along with us—she is a regular part of our demonology team—and she leaned forward and said to Ed, "Maybe I should have worn my crash helmet today." The winds were that bad. Later on I remember thinking that the winds were really a sign, a warning that we should stay away.

Q: Had you heard of the Smurls before?

Lorraine: No.

Q: You've mentioned that sometimes when you pull up to a house you get a feeling for the place right away. Did you get any particular feeling that day?

Ed: No, we sat in the car looking at the duplex and

the neighborhood. It was a pleasant day, even given the strong winds, and the neighborhood looked very peaceful. I kept watching Lorraine to see what was going through her mind as she looked around. But we really felt nothing untoward.

Q: Were you disappointed?

Lorraine: *(Laughing)* No, believe it or not, after three thousand investigations, we're quite happy when we find peaceful situations that stay that way.

Q: What was your first impression of the Smurls?

Lorraine: Well, that went along with our first impression of the house—very tranquil, very middle class, very upstanding.

Ed: That's the thing about many of the families we investigate where there is evidence of demonic infestation—we usually sense trouble right away.

Lorraine: Many of the families we deal with are experiencing problems outside the demonic. We find broken homes or couples on the brink of divorce or children so distraught they need to see psychiatrists. Usually you can understand how demons might settle on such families. We've learned that, in general, families who are having trouble with the supernatural run to a pattern—alcoholism or adultery or even outright child abuse—that enables the demonic to find a suitable place.

Q: You're saying the Smurls were not this way?

Lorraine: Not at all. Jack and Janet were very

hard-working, very honest people who had raised well-behaved and happy children.

Ed: We almost wondered if we'd found the right house.

Q: How did they explain their problems?

Ed: Well, since they'd moved in, many inexplicable events had taken place.

Q: Such as?

Lorraine: A good example would be what had happened after they remodeled their bathroom. They'd installed a new sink and bathtub and almost immediately afterward, they found talon marks over everything—as if a beast with claws had gone over everything.

Ed: Then there was a series of small but—to us—familiar examples of the demonic. Terrible odors filled the house. They would hear pounding and voices in empty rooms. And Dawn, their eldest daughter, saw people floating around near the ceiling of her room.

Q: What did the Smurls make of all this?

Lorraine: That was the trouble. They weren't sure how to account for it. Imagine this: You're a nice, normal middle-class family and all of a sudden all these terrible events start happening. How do you explain them? Do you tell other people about them? Won't other people think that you and your whole family are crazy?

Ed: Janet, who was often home alone during the day doing housework, became a particular target for these events. She would hear her name called and then she'd rush into the next room to see who was calling her and she'd find . . . nothing. One day she saw a black human-shaped figure that appeared to be wearing some kind of cape. The room she was in became very cold. She just stood there and watched it. She realized all of a sudden that she could see right through it.

Lorraine: But she remained calm. Janet and Jack are very strong people.

Ed: Yes, she let the demonic form pass right through her house and then she went next door to see how her mother-in-law Mary was doing. Mary startled her by admitting that she'd seen the same kind of form.

Q: So the infestation involved the entire family?

Ed: By this time, yes.

Q: How did you proceed?

Lorraine: Well, we were very cautious, as we always are. Sometimes things aren't what they seem. There's always the possibility that—for whatever reason—people are deceiving you.

Ed: But we took a team of psychic investigators and went through the house and that convinced us.

Q: What did you find?

Ed: We used an infrared camera and an audio tape recorder to see if we could find evidence of a demonic infestation.

Q: And you did find evidence?

Ed: Yes, we turned the lights out in the Smurl house and Lorraine and the rest of the team were in an upstairs bedroom. I took holy water and commanded the demons to be gone. We didn't have to wait long after that. Demons began pounding on the walls and tearing a mirror from a bureau and filling a TV set that was unplugged with some very eerie glows that bathed the whole room in color.

Lorraine: There was a terrible odor for a time too.

Q: So you had no doubt what you were dealing with?

Ed: None at all.

Q: Where did you proceed from there?

Lorraine: We tried to get the parish priest involved. Janet did, actually. But we didn't have any luck. The Catholic church is very conservative when it comes to matters involving the supernatural.

Q: How were things in the Smurl house?

Ed: Much worse. One thing about the diabolical—when you begin to challenge them, they have to assert their dominance. For example, a heavy lighting fixture fell from the ceiling and nearly killed one of the family. This was very dramatic, of course, and terrified everybody in the house, but so did the constant knocking in the walls and the bad odors and the demonic visions and the thefts.

Q: Things were stolen?

Lorraine: It's a form of terrorism. How demons like to move important items around and hide them or get rid of them permanently. The Smurls lost many valuable things in those days. Plus the children were more and more being bothered by the infestation.

Q: In what way?

Lorraine: Dawn Smurl, for example, was taking a shower when she felt a presence seize her arms and then brush up against her in an unmistakable way. It took all her strength to get from the shower to the hallway where she started screaming for her parents.

Ed: Yes, and Shannon—the Smurls have twin daughters, Shannon and Carin—was lured out of her bed and to the steep staircase one night and tripped down the stairs.

Lorraine: That really frightened the Smurls. Along with the ceiling fixture crashing down, the staircase incident demonstrated that these demons really meant to harm the family.

Ed: That was when we knew that a full exorcism was going to be necessary.

Q: Were you getting any more cooperation from the church?

Ed: Not really. We turned to Bishop Robert McKenna, who is a traditionalist priest, to help us.

Q: How did the exorcism go?

Ed: Well, right before then there was a terrifying incident. Jack Smurl was raped by a succubus.

Q: Would you describe that?

Ed: He was asleep in bed one night and he was awakened by this haglike woman who paralyzed him. He wanted to scream out, of course—he was horrified by what he saw, the woman had scales on her skin and white, scraggly hair, and some of her teeth were missing—but she paralyzed him in some manner. Then she mounted him and rode him to her sexual climax.

Q: Couldn't this have been a nightmare?

Ed: Oh, yes, very easily, except when the old woman finally disappeared and Jack staggered into the bathroom, he found himself covered by this very sticky substance that had been emitted from the creature's vagina.

Q: Did Janet Smurl hear any of this?

Ed: Sometimes, when it's hot at night, Janet goes down to sleep on the couch, which she'd done that night.

Q: Did Jack tell her what had happened?

Ed: Of course.

Q: How did she react?

Ed: Just the way you'd expect—she was horrified and terrified. But the rape didn't end there.

Q: No?

Ed: No. At breakfast in the morning Dawn Smurl told her father that she'd had a nightmare in which her father was attacked by this really ugly old woman with missing teeth and sores all over her body. Dawn had to be comforted at great length.

Q: How was the family holding up during all this?

Lorraine: It really depended on the day. Some days they were very positive and believed they could get through it all. But other days I'm sure they had doubts.

Ed: There's really nothing to prepare you for demonic infestation.

Lorraine: Even our own team of psychic investigators—which includes priests, police officers, nurses, and teachers—is depressed and frightened sometimes.

Ed: We've had team members quit right in the middle of investigations because they get so scared.

Lorraine: There was even a writer who refused to finish a piece on us because so many strange things began happening to him and his wife all of a sudden.

Q: He never finished the piece?

Ed: No; we never heard from him again.

Lorraine: His wife forbade it. She was pregnant at the time and afraid that something would happen to her child. I didn't blame her.

Q: Have you ever gotten so frightened that you wanted to quit?

Lorraine: Oh, sure. Lots of times, in fact. But we believe very deeply in our Catholic faith and believe deeply that what we're doing is performing a necessary service to the world.

Q: Were the Smurls appreciative of what you were doing?

Lorraine: Absolutely. We couldn't have asked for nicer people. They never complained; they just accepted their circumstances as a test of their faith.

Q: So you went ahead with the exorcism?

Ed: Yes. The first one was quite elaborate. It even had moments of beauty. Bishop McKenna is a very strong and courageous man.

Q: Was the ceremony successful?

Ed: For a time. In fact, we were happy to find out that afterward—when we were walking through the house searching for any signs of infestation—that the kitchen smelled of roses.

Lorraine: You should have seen the Smurls. Given the circumstances under which we'd met them, we'd never seen them truly happy before. But they certainly were following the exorcism.

Q: You sound almost euphoric now. You must have been really pleased then.

Lorraine: Oh, we were. Bishop McKenna had worked so hard—the fasting necessary for an exorcism is very difficult on people our age. And I suppose it was the way the children were smiling and laughing for the first time in months.

Q: How long did this last?

Lorraine: Unfortunately, only a few days.

Ed: We stayed in constant touch with the Smurls, so little by little we started hearing how their house was becoming infested again.

Q: What was going on?

Ed: Oh, the tapping sounds and the hissing sounds were back.

Lorraine: And the mother-in-law Mary Smurl had her duplex filled with the odor of raw sewage.

Ed: And Dawn saw earrings lifting from her jewelry box and flying around the room.

Lorraine: Then Janet woke up one morning with huge gouge marks in her arm. The marks were almost two inches long.

Q: So the demons were back.

Lorraine: Yes.

Q: How did the Smurls respond?

Ed: They started getting desperate. They wanted their own church people to take part, and when the church people refused, Janet went to the media.

Q: The story went worldwide, didn't it?

Lorraine: Definitely.

Q: And everything got reported?

Ed: Most of it. The black form had been walking through walls again and bringing trouble to both sides of the duplex, and certainly that got reported.

Lorraine: And of course the various media liked to settle on the most sensational aspects of the ordeal.

Q: Was the second exorcism reported?

Ed: (Nods) Yes, a few days after the second exorcism—two days of tranquillity for the Smurls—a golden woman, glowing woman really, appeared in the middle of the Smurl house and then vanished. Janet was alone at the time. She couldn't believe it. Here, for the second time, she'd gotten her hopes up again, and now everything was back to the familiar parts of the infestation.

Q: Did the Smurls ever try to escape the house?

Ed: That's one of the first questions most people ask. Why didn't they run away? Well, one time they did, in a sense, run away. They went camping to a state park.

Q: And what happened?

Ed: A demon followed them. It picked up a very heavy garbage can and hurled it at Jack.

Q: So there was no escape?

Ed: Not only was there no escape—there was a matter of pride involved. Jack Smurl is a hard-working man with no small degree of pride. He felt that this was his house—this was his family—and he darn well meant to protect them. And that's why he was so frustrated. Jack is the type of guy who believes in direct action. If you've got a problem, confront it, deal with it, and right now. But that's pretty hard to do when invisible spirits are calling the shots.

Q: Was there anything you could do?

Lorraine: Not anything other than what we were doing—lots of prayers, researching the house as much as we could—finding out about the previous occupants, for example, seeing if somebody there previously might not have "invited" the demons in—but other than that the Smurls were on their own.

Q: When did the media get involved?

Lorraine: Janet appeared on a TV show called "People Are Talking," and everything escalated from there.

Q: Wasn't there a newspaper interview?

Ed: Yes, this followed a second attack by the succubus on Jack.

Q: A second attack?

Lorraine: (Nods) Sometimes, in the case of possession, the demons get as frustrated as the people.

They want more and more control of the people they're haunting. This seemed to be the case here.

Ed: Yes, the demons were definitely escalating their attacks. Jack's legs were scalded by a heat that nothing could cool down except holy water. Then the phone started ringing all night—even when it was unplugged—keeping everybody up all night. And one night when Janet was lying on the couch a man with two animal horns protruding from his skull appeared intent on some kind of sexual contact. The only way she got rid of him was by dousing him with holy water.

Q: It sounds as if their lives had gone completely berserk.

Lorraine: Oh, yes. Definitely.

Ed: In fact, it got so bad there at times that the family became afraid to talk among themselves. They'd go out into the garage and whisper their plans to each other so the demons couldn't hear.

Q: Maybe the spotlight helped them.

Ed: It helped to this degree: The Smurls began receiving calls from other families who'd had problems with demons. At least the Smurls no longer felt alone or like freaks. They knew now that others had not only gone through this ordeal but survived it.

Lorraine: But they were also living in a fish bowl. Hundreds of spectators began camping out on their street, looking for a glimpse of the Smurls or of something strange going on in the house.

Ed: And not everybody was friendly.

Lorraine: That's right. Somebody threw a beer bottle through their front window.

Ed: And there were a lot of taunts—you know, the Smurls are crazy, the Smurls are making all of this up, the Smurls are just trying to draw attention to themselves. That sort of thing.

Lorraine: All this was especially tough on the children.

Q: Did all of this have an ending?

Ed: Well, supposedly it did.

Lorraine: But we really don't think so.

Ed: The Smurls moved finally, you see. They felt it was the only chance they had.

Q: And what happened?

Ed: For a while, everything seemed pretty good. There weren't any noises or any smells or any glimpses of demons.

Lorraine: But gradually they started again.

Q: Where are the Smurls now?

Ed: Essentially, they're in hiding.

Q: Hiding from what?

Lorraine: Right now, they're exhausted. They don't want any more publicity, any more scrutiny.

Q: I take it they're still being besieged by demons?

Lorraine: (Hesitates; looks sad) Let's just say they're not yet leading the lives they'd like to.

Ed: No; not at all.

The Smurl home has just very recently been successfully exorcised after permission was granted from a high Vatican source in Rome.

Case File:

THE UNSPEAKABLE

THIS is one case we'll never forget. What began as a routine investigation into some possible occult phenomena in Southern California became one of the strangest and most chilling cases of our entire lives.

Because of the subject matter, this is an investigation we don't often share with the public. While we feel that here all the facts can finally be presented to the reader, we want to warn you in advance: This is a deeply shocking story.

—Ed Warren

Milton Stone never told anybody where he went on Thursday nights—not even his eighty-one-year-old mother with whom he'd lived all his life except for a one-year stay at mortuary school in Omaha. Milton was now thirty-eight.

When he'd first started going out on Thursday nights—if his mother had had her way, he would *never* go out, not even to the Tomlin Funeral Home where Milton worked as a director—he'd worn disguises.

Sometimes he wore a red stocking cap and one of his dead father's old topcoats and a bushy mustache that he'd bought at a shop that sold theater items.

Other times he wore a Beatles wig he'd bought back in 1964 as a way to make people at his high school pay a little more attention to him. (The wig, like so many other risks he'd taken, only succeeded in making him seem even stranger to his classmates.)

A few times he even donned a jogging outfit and a gray toupee that fitted neatly over his balding head. In this get-up, he resembled an aging and overfed athlete.

Why all the disguises?

Because Milton didn't want to get caught.

By his mother (God forbid).

By his employer (the joke at the funeral home was that Rolfe Tomlin, Sr., got along with the dead people better than he did the living ones).

Or by his neighbors, who would be certain to tell (a) his mother and (b) Rolfe Tomlin.

So successful were his disguises that Milton was never caught.

Nobody in the neighborhood ever found out pathetic Milton's sweaty little secret: that he'd became a connoisseur of pornographic movies.

Not that this was Milton's first brush with pornography. Not at all.

Up in his bedroom closet, under a stack of boxes that contained the parts to the model airplanes that Milton had never been able to complete, lay a skin magazine. Milton figured he could get away with secreting one—but more than that would be just inviting discovery.

Milton used the magazine frequently, and not only for masturbation.

At night, with his elderly mother snoring down the hall, Milton took the magazine down and looked through it until he found the prettiest face.

Not the most ample breasts; not the most rounded buttocks.

The prettiest face.

Then he gave the face a name. (He hated the obviously phony names the magazines gave these women—Candy and Trixie and Wanda and names like that.) And always a gentle name.

Beth.

Susan.

Heather.

And then he'd lie back on his bed in his lonely little room and imagine himself married to Beth or Susan or Heather.

It wasn't just sex he imagined, though there was

a lot of that, and it was so rich and vital that it nearly drove him mad.

No; he also imagined an ordinary life with this woman. A suburban home. A night in front of the TV with popcorn. A walk through an October park, the colorful leaves stirring at their feet, a sweet chill wind balming them.

It was so sweet, so pure in its way.

Sometimes Beth or Susan or Heather would actually be Sandy Milligan, the girl from high school he'd loved so wildly and uselessly, always afraid to even so much as say hello to her.

But then his mother, waking up from one of her nightmares, would call out to him and the fantasy would fade and he would run down the hall, terrified that his mother would die, while a guilty part of him hoped she would die.

Then one day, walking home from the Tomlin Funeral Home, he passed by the sleazy but thrilling entranceway to a XXX movie house and something happened to him. He stood dumbstruck in the clamor of the late-spring afternoon, bus smoke and car horns and screaming children fading from his senses.

There was only one reality now—the life-size photograph of a very pretty, very sexy woman bent over in a most exciting way . . . and seeming to stare right at Milton.

This involved no fantasies of suburban homes or popcorn nights in front of the TV or walks through the park.

This was raw sex at its most overwhelming.

Milton had never felt more confused.

Wasn't he old enough and responsible enough to make up his own mind about going inside?

Yes.

But wasn't he equally afraid of what his mother would do if she ever found out?

Yes.

He could imagine her carrying on.

Sobbing.

Screaming.

Clutching her heart and telling him she probably had only a few moments left.

And then snatching her special crucifix from the bureau (as a girl, she'd visited Rome, and the Pope had blessed this crucifix personally) and holding it out in front of herself like a victim in a horror movie holding it out to a vampire.

Learning he'd gone to an X-rated movie house might well kill her.

How would he ever live with such guilt?

Quickly, before he did something he might regret, he forced himself away from the theater.

A few blocks later, as the sexual tension that had gripped him began to subside, he had his first thought about disguise.

As a boy, one of his favorite TV shows was *The Wild, Wild West*. Even though his mother many times expressed displeasure with the half-naked women who were always offering themselves to Special Agent Jim West, Milton watched as often as he could.

His favorite part of the show was when Artemus

Ward, so ably played by Ross Martin, donned a disguise and went undercover. Sometimes his disguises fooled even Jim West, played by Robert Conrad.

The next night, wearing his Beatles wig and a pair of horn-rimmed glasses and the theater-shop mustache, Milton attended his first pornographic movie.

He thought of it as an electric cave, Milton did.

He sat in the back row with the jumbo buttered popcorn and the jumbo Coca-Cola (no diet stuff on porno nights; the real thing) and then he just gave himself up to the magical technicolor images that moved so erotically on the wall of the cave before him.

All his life, Milton had dreamed of possessing women in the way they were possessed in these movies.

He sat there, unmindful of all others in this cave, sweating, writhing, moaning as the images danced across the wall, offering him the wet and sensuous glimpses of women he had never known before.

He went to the pornographic movies twenty-four Thursday nights in a row.

He confessed his sin, of course, in the anxious darkness of the confessional, the priest's breath old and oniony on the other side of the cloth; the church dark as the movie house when he knelt saying his penance.

Sometime around the eighteenth week, his mother became suspicious.

"I mark it down."

"You mark what down, Mother?"

"When you go."

"When I go where?"

"When you go where? Just because I'm old doesn't mean that I'm stupid, does it?"

"No, Mother."

"You go somewhere you're not supposed to go."

"How do you know that?"

"Because in the middle of the night on Thursday nights I carry my holy candle into your room and watch you on your bed. While you're sleeping, your whole body twitches. You look like an old person who's dying."

"I go bowling."

"Bowling. You expect me to believe that?" She fixed him with her dark crone's eye. "It's a girl, isn't it?"

He blushed. Ever since he was very little, his mother had had a way of saying the world "girl" that brought almost intolerable shame upon him. "No," he said. "I promise. It's not a girl."

The crone's eye examined his face with X-ray scrutiny.

"Then where do you go?"

"Bowling."

"Pah."

"And after bowling, I go for a walk. Haven't you noticed that my waistline is getting smaller?"

"Pah. It's bigger. I've had to let out all your trousers in the past month. It's a girl, isn't it?"

"No," he said, and not knowing what else to do, went to his room.

She stood on the other side of his closed door. "It's a girl! I know it's a girl!" she shouted.

He covered his head with a pillow so he would not have to listen to her.

Finally she went away.

To say that Milton Stone had never seen a naked woman before would not be technically telling the truth.

In fact, Milton had seen lots of naked women.

The problem was, these were naked *dead* women.

As part of his job as funeral director, Milton helped with the process of embalming. The first few times he'd participated, he'd felt as if he were working in a slaughterhouse on the killing floor.

One comes to know that human beings are meat—just as beef and pigs are meat—when one works in a funeral home.

The soul may be beautiful and soar upward to be one with God the Father and Jesus the Son and the Holy Spirit, but the body remains a frail, and quickly rotting, vessel that only briefly houses what we call life.

Most of the time he worked with corpses, Milton had a way of not exactly *looking* at them.

Oh, he was aware of what he was doing—he was even expert at it—but he certainly didn't let his eyes dwell on any part of the naked bodies.

For one thing, it was sinful.

Flesh was, alas, flesh, dead or living.

For another it was eerie.

Sometimes Milton expected the people on whom he was working to sit up and start laughing and say it was all a joke.

There's no such thing as death, Milton.

We were just fooling.

Milton even had dreams that such things happened. Perhaps the little joke was a way of keeping his distance from the reality he faced every day.

Then he saw the twenty-four-year-old young woman who had died of natural causes.

Her full breasts and womanly hips reminded him of the women he saw in the X-rated movies.

He could not believe—indeed tried to deny—the feelings that overwhelmed him.

That spring, Ed and Lorraine Warren were enjoying particular success as guests on the talk-show circuit.

They were also compiling their amazing record of painstakingly investigating more than two thousand cases of the supernatural throughout North America, Europe, and Australia. In addition, they were teaching courses on demonology and paranormalogy to college audiences coast to coast.

All this considered, the call they got from a very shy woman might have gone unnoticed. The woman talked about a brother who was behaving strangely. The brother lived at home with his mother. Then the woman said something that made the Warrens take particular note of her: "Last Sunday my brother levitated."

"Did your mother tell you this?" Ed asked.

"No, I was sitting ten feet away. I saw it for myself."

Ed and Lorraine Warren became very interested in the retiring young woman and her remarkable brother.

"Don't you love me?"

"Yes. And that's why your sister and I invited them here."

"If you loved me, you wouldn't let strange people come and examine me."

"They're just trying to help."

Milton and his mother had been having this argument all day.

He did not understand why his sister Rosalind had contacted the Warrens, the couple she'd seen on Mike Douglas.

"It's the devil's work," the mother said again. "You can't imagine what it was like. You were lying down right on that couch over there. Asleep—and then your whole body began rising through the air."

As usual, she sat in the living room in an ancient, dusty dress, dark paisley but faded, with a high frilly white collar and an enormous brooch at the neck. Her hair was gray and so severely combed, it looked almost wiglike. Her gnarled knuckles sat upon the handle of her walking stick.

"I don't want them here."

"You're keeping something from me, Milton. Something is going on."

"Nothing's going on. I'm overworked is all. Stress."

"This is the devil's work," she said again.

Milton went in and closed his door.

He covered his hands with his face.

What if the Warrens weren't the frauds he half expected them to be?

What if they had some way of finding out what Milton had been doing? . . .

The Warrens flew to the West Coast . . .

"Milton, these are the Warrens."

Milton stood next to the dining-room table.

Though he was grossly overweight, his starched white shirt and dark trousers reminded Lorraine of the clothes a youngster might wear to take his first communion.

In an almost sinister way, there *was* something boyish about Milton.

"Hello," Milton said.

"We'd just like to talk to you," Ed said easily. "About what happened here last week."

"I think they imagined it," Milton said.

"You do?"

Milton shrugged. "They've been worried about me. It would stand to reason, wouldn't it?"

"What would stand to reason?"

Milton shrugged again. He had started sweating heavily even though it was cool in the room. "Them worrying would make them invent things."

"Not necessarily," Ed said.

Rosalind, the thin, attractive sister, said, "Why don't we sit down and have some of the coffee and apple pie I made?"

Everybody sat down.

Milton looked like a six-year-old who was being punished for not eating his vegetables.

For the first twenty minutes of the interview, he was sulky and uncooperative. He became pleasant only when his aged mother began sending him warning signs with her dark, liquid eyes—in a raven's eyes, Ed thought.

Ed says, "We interviewed Milton on six different occasions before I really started to understand what was going on here. With each interview, Milton drew more and more into himself. By this time, we had no doubt that he'd levitated. We also had no doubt that his mother was right—that what we were witnessing here was the work of satanic forces.

"Milton obviously had something to hide. This is a problem we run into quite frequently. We go into a home and ask if anything odd has taken place to any of the family members over the past few months— and the answer is almost always no.

"People are just afraid to talk. Sometimes this is because of their natural reluctance to reveal family secrets, even if those secrets aren't damaging or embarrassing. But other times, people know they've really got something to hide and so they tell us nothing.

"This was the case with Milton. Here was a man who obviously had something to hide, but he sure wasn't going to tell us about it without a struggle."

After the sixth interview, during which the sister had reported another instance of levitation and the mother had reported more instances of hearing strange voices coming from Milton's room, Ed and Lorraine began working on an explanation for all this that genuinely shocked them.

"At first, we rejected the whole notion," Ed says. "It seemed not only improbable, it seemed almost sinful to even think about. While we'd heard of such cases, we'd never actually encountered one ourselves."

For the seventh interview, Ed arranged for a videotape camera to be brought along. He had convinced the family that he wanted to tape their apartment because sometimes infrared tape could pick up sights the human eye could not.

What Ed really wanted to do was subtly intimidate Milton with the camera. When he sensed the camera eye on him—Ed planned to suggest casually they go ahead and tape the interview—maybe Milton would start to feel pressure and begin to talk honestly about what had been going on in his life.

"Do you like your job, Milton?" Ed asked.

"Yes."

"Have you ever thought of any other line of work?"

"No."

"Is there a lot of pressure?"

"Sometimes, when two or three funerals get booked in the same day."

"How about dealing with dead people?"

"You mean does it bother me?"

"Yes."

"No, it doesn't. I'm used to it."

"I would think that embalming people could get pretty grim sometimes."

"It depends on the case."

"In what respect?" Ed asked.

"Well, certainly it's very sad when a young child has died. Even funeral directors, who really have to learn to accept death, have trouble with young children. I've seen my boss break down and cry when he's had to bury a child."

"But ordinarily, working with corpses doesn't bother you?"

"Not usually. A bad car accident might. Something really grisly."

"But the run-of-the-mill—"

"No."

Ed paused. "Have you ever heard of funeral directors who took certain liberties with the people they buried?"

"Certain liberties?"

"Sexual liberties."

"No; no, I haven't."

"I'm told it happens sometimes."

"Really?"

"Yes."

"Well, that's certainly a disgusting subject to bring up, especially in my own home, with my mother and sister just in the next room."

Ed was now watching Milton's face very carefully.

"Do you ever work with attractive women?" Ed asked.

"You mean dead women who are attractive?"

"Yes."

"Sometimes."

"And so you see them naked?"

"Of course."

"Have you ever felt any carnal desire for them?"

"Of course not."

Milton's entire body was slick with sweat. He trembled and he kept biting on his lower lip. "What are you trying to say?"

"Just that people don't start levitating for no reason."

"I didn't want them to invite you here."

"I sensed that, Milton."

"What goes on in my life is none of your business."

"Calm down, Milton."

"Why should I calm down? This is my home and you're sitting here asking me filthy questions."

"Would you like a glass of water?"

"No."

"Would you like me to get your mother in here so you might calm down a little?"

"No."

Ed paused. "Milton?"

"Yes."

"Sometimes when we commit a sin that's particularly bad, we invite demons into our lives."

"I go to mass three times a week."

"I know you do."

"I say my rosary every night."

"I know that too."

"I'm not a bad man."

"I'm sure you're not."

Milton pointed to the camera. "Why is that on?"

"I just thought I might like to study it later."

"Why?"

"Because sometimes the camera sees things we can't."

"Such as what?"

"Oh, demons, to use a simple term."

"The camera picks up things you can't?"

"Sometimes."

This answer seemed to appease Milton. He turned to the window and stared glumly outdoors.

"I don't know how you could even think I could do such a thing," Milton said.

"I'm trying to help you, Milton. I'm your friend, not your enemy."

"The women I see naked—" He hesitated.

"Yes, Milton?"

"Sometimes they look—" He hesitated again.

"Yes?"

"I admit that sometimes they look erotic."

"They do?"

"Yes, that part I admit. But I've never—"

"You've never what?"

"Never—touched them."

"In any way?"

Milton shook his head.

"Is there anything else you want to say, Milton?"

Tears formed in Milton's eyes and began running down his plump cheeks.

Milton made small, useless fists of his hands and began pounding them hard into his thighs.

Ed knew that Milton was confessing to having

had sex with some of the corpses he worked on. It
was just that he couldn't quite get the words out.

"You have to be strong, Milton," Ed said.

"I know."

"Even though you've done things you're ashamed
of, it's not too late to stop."

"I know."

"You can get rid of the demons if you want to."

Milton cried more freely now. "I can?"

"Yes."

"My nightmares—" He began sobbing like a
young boy. "In my nightmares I see these dead
women—naked women—coming for me—angry for
what I did—"

"It's not too late to stop, Milton. Your mother
and your sister love you very much. You can draw
strength from them, Milton."

Ed let Milton sit there and cry.

Finally, after five minutes or so, Ed got up
quietly and went into the living room and beckoned
to the mother and the sister. "Why don't you come in
and talk with Milton awhile now?"

"Did you make some progress today?" Rosalind
asked.

"Oh, yes," Ed said solemnly. "We made some
progress today."

"As lurid as this story is, it illustrates a simple,
dramatic fact that never leaves our minds. However

sordid the circumstances, at the center of all demonic incidents is a human being in great trouble," Lorraine says.

Milton, while not the sort of human being most of us would find appealing in any way, was still at heart a decent man just trying to live out a life that was terribly lonely and confusing.

He turned to perhaps the worst sin of all—necrophilia—and in so doing, handed his life over to the devil.

His struggle to free himself from his torment goes on to this day.

Case File:

THE
DARKNESS
AFTER

LORRAINE and I have been involved in many cases where an inquisitive teenager virtually (and in some cases literally) invites demonic spirits into a house, but the one in upstate New York was one of the most troubling because it had aspects of the comic to it.

The girl is now in her mid-twenties and the mother of two, but it's unlikely she'll ever forget what happened to her once she started reading paperback novels on the demonic.

—Ed Warren

Maybe it was her breath, Mandy Robison thought to herself. Maybe it was bad and she didn't even know it.

Or maybe it was the new perfume she was using.

Whatever it was, her sudden lack of popularity with her friends in eleventh grade was getting hard to explain.

Here was a pretty and friendly sixteen-year-old who only two weeks earlier had been one of the most popular girls in her class and then—

Then her boyfriend of eleven months suddenly broke up with her.

Then her manager at the McDonald's where she worked after school decided to take her from the counter and stick her in the back where nobody could see her.

As if he were ashamed of her or something.

So what was it? Bad breath? The wrong perfume? A sudden case of leprosy that she was the last to know about?

At this point, Mandy made no connection between the books she'd been reading lately and the sudden downturn in her social fortunes.

But a quick glance at her bookcase showed her to have most peculiar reading tastes.

On the first shelf you found such titles as *The Compleat Warlock; Satan Is My Friend;* and *My Nights with Demons*. To say nothing of the second shelf, which included such masterpieces as: *Contacting the Other Realm; Fifteen Weeks in Hell;* and *Knowing the Darkness*.

During a baby-sitting job the past summer, Mandy had started reading whatever paperbacks the Folsoms had lying around their somewhat messy house. The Folsoms had seemed to have a genuine interest in occult matters, hence all these really weird books on other worlds beyond our own.

The thing was, Mandy took these tomes largely as jokes. She loved to leaf through them, stumble upon some incantation that would supposedly open the gates of hell, and then speak the incantation aloud until she found herself laughing so hard that tears rolled down her cheeks.

Good clean harmless fun.

But then all of a sudden her friends started finding reasons to not be her friends anymore.

What was going on here?

"There was just something about her. I'm not even sure I can explain it," a young man named Roland Klever explains to the interviewer. "Here she was, this really cute girl that most of the boys really wanted to date, but then something changed about her.

"I remember seeing her going down the hall one day and there was this very dark aura around her. It shone on her face and made her look like this real old hag. But when you'd blink the aura would be gone and Mandy would be her old self again.

"I wasn't the only one who saw it. Her boyfriend Jack saw it too. That's why he broke up with her. He really got afraid. People were whispering about her all the time but she didn't seem to catch on."

Cathy Miles, a bright, attractive woman who was once Mandy's best friend, later revealed: "I was out for an after-school walk with Mandy one day and I saw her change shape. Literally. She became this demon. I didn't scream—I was afraid I was losing my mind or hallucinating and I figured that if I screamed, that would only call attention to my problem. But then I started talking to other kids— and they started seeing strange things happening around Mandy too."

Mandy first became aware of her difficulty when she was walking home with a nine-year-old boy named Clint trailing behind her.

Clint had had a terrible crush on Mandy for the past year. He often asked Mandy if she believed in younger men and older women having affairs. Mandy always smiled to herself and said no.

On her way home from school one afternoon, Clint riding several feet behind her on his Schwinn, Mandy turned to face the boy—only to watch him scream like somebody in a sci-fi movie who'd just seen a monster.

He started pedaling back the way he'd come, obviously afraid to even turn around.

Stunned, and suspicious, Mandy stood staring after the boy for several long minutes.

She thought of how strangely other people had been acting, too.

What was going on here, anyway?

She walked on home.

That night, when she was daubing some Clearasil on a zit, she finally realized why all her friends—and even lovesick Clint—had been acting so peculiarly around her.

That night, in the mirror, she saw the old hag the others glimpsed—pus running from sores that looked like moon craters, red eyes that cast an eerie glow, teeth that were no more than blackened stubs, and warts that turned outward at odd and disgusting angles.

When her parents found her, she was lying naked on the bathroom floor, sobbing and screaming and rolling back and forth as if in the power of some invisible force.

"Mrs. Warren?"

"Yes."

"My name is Alma Robison. I was referred to you by Father Hallahan."

"Oh, yes. How is Father Hallahan? We haven't seen him for a while."

"He's fine." Pause. "I'm calling about my daughter. She's—having some problems."

"What sort of problems, Mrs. Robison?"

"Well, she thinks she's become haunted in some way."

Mrs. Robison then went on to explain about the occult books Mandy had been reading. And about the strange behavior of her friends.

Lorraine listened patiently and then said, "Has she been experimenting with the incantations in these books, Mrs. Robison?"

The mother, as parents usually do, sounded a bit defensive. "Well, she was really treating it as a joke, Mrs. Warren—I mean, she wasn't taking this seriously. But now—last night I heard her scream and I ran up to her room."

"Did you find anything?"

"I couldn't see anything but her room was very cold. Very cold. And it was a nice warm spring night."

"Could you describe the cold you felt?"

"All I can think of is a meat locker. You know, how you walk into a locker and you start shivering right away?"

As Lorraine knew only too well, this was often a sure sign of demonic infestation. The presence of sudden cold many times meant that a demon was making its presence known to the person who had given it permission to take form.

"Did Mandy explain why she was screaming?"

"She said she felt hands running up and down her body. As if—well, in a sexual way. Do you understand?"

"Where is Mandy now?"

"I kept her home from school today. She's upstairs sleeping. Is there any way you could drive up and visit with her?"

"Yes. Right away. We'll be there this afternoon."

Mrs. Robison sighed. "There's something else, Mrs. Warren."

"Yes."

"I went and got my Bible and went into her room and started reading and—"

Pause.

"And I felt the hands too. All over my body. In the same sexual way. The whole family's scared, Mrs. Warren. We just don't know what to do."

Mrs. Robison then started crying.

Lorraine Warren comforted her as well as she could and promised that she and Ed would be there as soon as possible.

"Please hurry," Mrs. Robison said. "Please hurry."

That afternoon Lorraine and Ed Warren found a very troubled family waiting for them in a well-kept if modest suburban home.

Mr. Robison, a large man who worked as a

factory foreman, sat in the front room. He scarcely greeted them. He seemed embarrassed that the Warrens had come, even more embarrassed when his wife began relating other experiences that she had been reluctant to discuss over the phone.

● Mandy had been having conversations with an eighteen-year-old boy who had been dead for many years and who had come to her following one of her incantations. The boy's spirit constantly whispered sexual words to the girl and told her how much he would like to know her carnally.

● Mandy, in an effort to dispel this spirit, had taken her own Bible to her room only to have it ripped from her hands and torn into many pieces.

● In the middle of the night a week ago, the demonic hands found Mandy again and this time began to go up inside her. When Mandy resisted, the spirit flung her from her bed and began beating her, so badly that her body was covered with scars and bruises.

● While she was resting the next day, the spirit began touching her breasts and whispering foul words to Mandy, taunting her to join with other spirits in the next realm.

● The second time Mandy experienced the icy coldness in her room, she began to get glimpses of terrible creatures, some without eyes and noses, some with open, running wounds, moving around her room and making sexual threats.

"She's up in her room now," Mrs. Robison said.

Still looking embarrassed, Mr. Robison said, "Couldn't all this just be her imagination?"

"It could," Lorraine Warren said gently. "But getting thrown around her room would indicate that something is going on."

Mr. Robison nodded glumly.

They all went upstairs to see Mandy.

The girl before them had lost fifteen pounds in the past three weeks. Lack of sleep had carved deep rings beneath her eyes. In sweaty pajamas, she huddled in the corner of her bed as if expecting an attack at any moment.

Great fear shone in her pale blue eyes as she greeted the Warrens.

"May I see the books you've been reading?" Lorraine said.

Mandy pointed tentatively to her bookcase.

Lorraine went over and examined the books. As she thumbed through them, she saw certain key passages underlined. Most of these consisted of invitations to make demonic spirits a part of one's life.

Lorraine looked back at the Robisons. "Would

you leave Ed and me alone with Mandy for a while?"

The Robisons glanced at each other and then back to Lorraine. They nodded. Mrs. Robison went over and kissed Mandy on the forehead. Then the Robisons went downstairs.

For the rest of the daylight hours, Lorraine and Ed talked to the young girl. They found out the nature of the spirit who had been giving her so much trouble and then they learned more details of how the spirit had been manifesting itself.

At one point, Ed excused himself and went downstairs to talk to the parents. He asked if he might call a priest he knew. The Robisons agreed.

Ed then went into the kitchen and phoned Father Chambers, a young priest who, despite the reluctance of his bishop, had become interested in the supernatural. He got in his car at once and came over.

Upstairs, the Warrens and the priest asked the girl to lie very still and to keep a rosary in her hand. They then set about summoning up the demon who had possessed her.

It did not take long.

The girl began to cry and scream. Terrible taunts came from her lips. This was the demon speaking.

Over the next half hour, the trio spoke to the

demon and confirmed what Mrs. Robison had told them, that the spirit belonged to an eighteen-year-old boy who had died while struggling with his father. Always violent in life, the boy had found himself to be a violent spirit in death. He hoped to possess Mandy carnally and to enslave her in any way he could.

A fetid stench rose in the room.

They watched as invisible hands tore at Mandy's hair and hurled her from the bed.

But no matter what the spirit did to her, Mandy continued to grasp her rosary.

Lorraine took the occult books Mandy had been reading to the bathroom and burned them in the sink.

When she returned, she joined hands with Ed and Father Chambers in praying for the girl who was now back on her bed, trembling and crying out for blankets.

The room had become icy cold once more.

Midnight came and still the prayers continued.

From time to time, the Robisons crept up the stairs and went to their daughter's door, knocking softly to ask how things were going.

As yet, the Warrens didn't know how things were going.

Night gave way to dawn and dawn to the noisy hustle of a new day as people left for school, for work, for an idle day of pleasure.

But in the tiny bedroom of the small suburban house where a priest and two demonologists continued their work, there was neither night nor day.

There was just prayer.

Lorraine said, "Mandy went through all the transformations we're accustomed to seeing. When the spirit had been temporarily isolated and Mandy was herself, she was sweet and helpful. But when the demon took over, she changed completely—her innocent young face was ugly and haggard and old and she called us every sort of name imaginable and demanded that we leave."

Even the priest, good as his intentions were, began to weaken. There is no work as physically demanding as dealing with a demon. Because they are not of human flesh, demons are tireless. Father Chambers was exhausted.

The Warrens helped him to a chair in the corner and continued for a time saying the prayers themselves.

Then the priest, rested from his brief respite, rejoined them and once more led the prayers.

In Latin, in English, in formal prayers, in emotional pleas, the trio asked God to help them save the spiritual and physical life of this young girl.

These were prayers as old as the cosmic darkness that Lucifer knew as home.

These were prayers heard in the catacombs when the early Christians were beset not only by Romans but by Satan's legions as well.

These were prayers that had banished the dark

shapes of the Druids from their midnight altars of stone dripping with the sacrificial blood of virgins.

O Lord, spare this life.

O Lord, be with us here in this room.

O Lord, give our hearts hope and satisfaction.

Around three o'clock that afternoon, Mandy Robison began weeping in such a way that the Warrens and Father Chambers knew the demon had at last been banished.

These were the tears of innocence, of joy that the soul had once again joined Jesus.

"I wish I could say that Mandy Robison lived happily forever after," Lorraine Warren says on a bright winter morning with hills of snow sparkling in her window.

"Unfortunately, demonic infestation doesn't work that way. You can never quite be sure that you've really driven out the demon.

"In Mandy's case, she went on to finish high school, attend two years of college, get married and start a family of her own—before the demon was in evidence again.

"Mandy, who usually writes us once or twice a year, had what her family physician called a 'nervous breakdown.' But we were suspicious. We visited Mandy in the psychiatric hospital.

"All the same manifestations were there—the

hideous faces, the sexual taunts, the icy cold room.

"Her husband let us and Father Chambers—who was still in the area and who had by now performed many exorcisms, though not with the approval of his diocese—join Mandy again in trying to drive out the demons.

"At this point, things are going well for Mandy. She's back home, her husband was recently promoted in his job, and Mandy's oldest daughter just celebrated her eighth birthday.

"Right now Mandy is having no more problems. We certainly hope she's seen the last of that eighteen-year-old boy she inadvertently called up by reading those incantations."

Ed: "This is a case we always cite because it demonstrates exactly why you should not trifle with other realms. As Lorraine notes, we have only hope to go on where Mandy is concerned. Sometimes a person's life goes on for years without any trouble showing up and then— We've known several cases of so-called suicide that were actually the last resort of people trying to deal with demonic possession; they simply took what looked to them like the easiest way out."

Case File:

THE TERRIFIED MINISTER

MOST *people assume that minis-*
ters, priests, and rabbis are not usually the
targets of demonic spirits but, as the following
case illustrates, many people of the cloth see
their lives become enmeshed in—even con-
trolled by—the supernatural.

This particular case also illustrates an-
other point—that a haunting can last many
years. Here we have an example of phenomena
taking place over more than a century, involv-
ing literally dozens of lives.

—Ed Warren

The year was 1850. The place Stratford, Connecticut.

The Revolutionary War ended, New England was now setting about the real business of America—business. Stratford was no exception. Smoke from industry and the clatter of wagons loaded down with dry goods were common sights.

Except on Sunday mornings.

Like many other small New England towns, Stratford was a place filled with churches. You could take your choice, depending on your particular beliefs.

One of the most popular ministers in the town was the Reverend Elijah Phelps. Though he was not a shouter or a pulpit-pounder, Phelps was considered one of the most effective speakers in all of New England. Some said it was his low, authoritative voice. Others said it was his piercing gaze. Still others argued that it was his aura of righteousness coupled with compassion that made him so effective in the pulpit.

Whatever the exact reason for his popularity, Phelps usually found his church packed on Sunday mornings.

Indeed, he sometimes wondered if he wasn't a little too popular—was it seemly for a man of the cloth to have such a following?

In addition to his church activities, Phelps also spent a great deal of time studying the intellectual magazines and books of his era. In the New England tradition that combined the spiritual with the aesthetic, the Reverend Phelps sought to know both the ways of God and man.

It was rumored, therefore, that Phelps did not put much faith in the occult. He considered this realm to be neither intellectual nor spiritual—but to be largely the province of charlatans.

His skepticism changed one Sunday morning after he'd returned, with his wife and two children, from Sunday services. On March 14, 1850, the good Reverend Phelps, along with his wife and two children, walked into his home—and his life was never the same again.

The Phelps family lived in a large, Federal-style mansion that was literally the envy of the town. On Sundays, many people drove by in their buggies, or strolled by in couples, for a better look at the beautiful home.

At the moment, however, it wasn't so beautiful.

Not inside, anyway.

The place looked as if a pillaging army had marched through it.

Fine pottery, elegant draperies, lovely paintings—all had been hurled to the floor and destroyed.

Furniture had been torn apart and smashed.

Clothes from the closet had been hurled into piles and then torn with clawlike fury.

What was going on here?

Then the Reverend Phelps ventured into the parlor. What he saw there brought an instant prayer to his lips.

Only God could explain such a lurid and startling mockery as Phelps saw displayed before him.

Sitting in a semicircle were eleven life-size dummies dressed in colonial-era clothes. The dummies had their hands folded in prayer and their eyes raised to—

—a chandelier above, from which was suspended the image of a dwarf whose face had been covered with lewd markings.

Stunned, the Phelps family fled their home, standing outside in the fresh air of the otherwise peaceful Sunday, trying to determine what was going on.

Later on, after they had gone back inside the house, the family was to hear strange knockings and strange noises that came from the shadowy interiors of closets and to see familiar objects fly around the house.

That night the Phelps family slept together in a single bed, huddled against the onslaught of the demonic that they knew had visited their home.

Following that Sunday, rappings and screaming sounds could be heard during the black hours of night.

None were ever explained.

In a fit of courage, the Reverend Phelps once took a small torch and investigated every nook and cranny in the house.

He turned up nothing.

The rappings and screaming continued.

Phelps became a more deeply religious man. Where before he had shown at least a modicum of pride in his abilities as a preacher, people now noticed a new humility settled over the man.

His experiences with the occult—and the effects these experiences had had on his family—had taught him the true meaning of Jesus' words . . . and a real awe for the unseen forces that operate throughout the cosmos.

Eventually the Phelps family left the area. Rumors about the house did not leave with them. Indeed, townspeople seemed to take a perverse pride in the place.

The house became one of the few buildings to be written up in various travel journals as haunted.

People came from far away to see it. Trains often brought Sunday visitors eager for a glimpse of the mansion. Omnibuses were packed with tourists eager for the tiniest proof that the Federal-style house was in fact haunted.

Listen, is that a scream I hear?

Look, is that a ghost?

Over the years, townspeople learned to laugh gently about the Phelps place.

The rappings and screaming went from being sinister to being familiar and somehow friendly, like a wild animal that had been tamed to become a pet.

The Phelps home had become an honest-to-goodness tourist attraction.

Years became decades and decades became years. History was played out in the town of Stratford just as it was played out across the rest of the land.

World War I became World War II and World War II became Korea and Vietnam.

John F. Kennedy burned so brightly in the darkness of time and then fell into shadows and silence.

Stratford itself yielded to modern tastes while being sensible enough to keep much of the architecture and the artifacts that made its history so unique.

The old Phelps home served a variety of uses, the last of which was to be a home for the elderly.

No longer did eager Sunday visitors stroll by or drive by in Model-Ts for a glimpse of its darkened windows.

No longer were stories told of the eerie noises

you heard there when the moon was high and beasts walked the land.

Oh, little boys still liked to tell tales of what they suspected went on there. Nothing beats being scared when you're over at a friend's house for Friday night.

But mostly the place was forgotten . . . except for curious stories about nunlike figures appearing in the windows of the mansion from time to time.

Elderly people thankful for a home sat on its wide porches in rockers.

Nurses in crisp white uniforms came and went.

And not a single knock or a single scream was heard, even when the full harvest moon was blood red and when the host of the local monster movie assured us that Dracula was on the prowl.

But all this changed with the appearance of a local policeman sent to investigate strange noises heard by passersby.

Having been a policeman for nearly twenty years, the detective realized that most such calls usually had the same result—you generally found kids playing in a deserted house.

But even as he drove up to the crumbling, now-deserted mansion, the detective sensed something different about this call.

He wasn't sure why his hands had begun to twitch.

Or why his body had begun to sweat.

There was just something . . .

Taking his heavy-duty flashlight, the detective approached the old Phelps place carefully.

Over the years, windows had been broken and various kinds of debris scattered over the lawn, making the approach treacherous in the dark.

When he reached the porch, he tried the knob on the front door, found it locked, and went around to the side. While he was walking, he thought he saw something flash inside—nothing he could define or describe . . . just some sort of presence that flashed in the moonlight.

He assumed he'd gotten his first glimpse of the kid or kids who had entered the house and were now playing inside.

Around back, he found one of the rear entrance doors open. Clutching the light tighter in his gloved hand, he proceeded inside.

The first thing he noticed was the temperature. It felt thirty degrees colder in here than it did outside.

He started shivering immediately.

Moonlight washed the vast kitchen. In the days of the Reverend Phelps, a small staff had prepared meals there for the minister and his family.

In the days of the home for the elderly, a larger staff had prepared cafeteria-style meals for the old folks who had lived there.

Now the place was a dusty, cobwebbed place of ancient food smells, creaking noises in the battered walls, and the numbing cold that lay over the entire house.

Working his light before him, the detective went into the rest of the house. All the dust soon played havoc with his allergies. Not even the cold stopped the particles from plugging up his sinuses.

The detective spent the first twenty minutes checking out everything on the ground floor.

Closets creaked open and the light splashed in; bulky furniture was pushed aside and the light played over empty walls; doors leading into other rooms were eased open and the light trained on more dusty furniture.

Nothing.

Nothing that could be seen or heard anyway.

But still the detective knew that something was in this house.

Something.

If it was a teenager—or, even more unlikely, multiple teens—then he was the quietest teenager the detective had ever known.

Now he trained his light on the broad sweeping staircase that disappeared into the gloom of the second floor.

He gulped.

Despite all the pep talks he'd been giving himself about there being no such thing as ghosts, actually being in the old Phelps place was another matter entirely.

You heard certain things.

Or thought you did.

You saw certain things.

Or thought you did.

And you sensed—

Eyes.

There was no other way to put it.

You sensed eyes watching you.

Waiting.

He shone his light on the stair again and took his first step up into the darkness above.

What was that?

His head jerked backward as he thought he heard—

But no.

Nothing.

Needed to get control of himself.

Back up the staircase.

One hand on the banister.

One around the flashlight.

Dust worse than ever.

Coughing.

Sneezing.

And then he got his first good glimpse of the thing.

When you've been a policeman as long as this particular officer, you don't often get afraid of much. Guns in the hands of criminals scare you and maybe a butcher knife in the clutch of an enraged and drunken husband. But not much else.

With the exception of something not . . . human . . . running down a hallway at the top of a darkened staircase.

What had he seen?

Now in addition to the terrible cold, the detective also smelled something . . . foul.

He went on up the stairs.

It was his job.

And anyway, wasn't he being silly? Letting the reputation of an aged house overcome his best instincts and better judgment?

Wasn't he . . . ?

Just at the edge of the circle where his light played, he saw it again.

Whatever it was.

A dark figure, slight in build, short in stature . . . running down the hall.

When he reached the top of the staircase, the detective started running.

He was vaguely afraid he would trip over something and break some bones. But he kept running.

In the shadows of the wide, dusty hallway he saw the outline of the figure in the moonlight through the cobwebbed windows.

"Stop!" he shouted, and pulled his Smith and Wesson .38.

But the figure kept running.

And now it was making vague noises, almost chittering noises.

Noises that were terrifying.

The detective dove into the last room on this west side of the hall, the same room he'd seen the small figure enter.

Now the detective found himself in a large, empty room with a long-dead fireplace on the east wall. Obviously at one time, more than a hundred years ago, this had been the master bedroom.

The detective's footsteps were loud in the eerie silence. He raised his flashlight, shone it through swirling dust motes, and trained it on a closet door.

The figure had to have run in there.

The detective was certain the figure had come in this room. Therefore, there was only one place the figure could hide.

Therefore, the figure had to be in the—

—closet.

Heart pounding, the detective moved forward.

His shoe leather squeaked.

Far, far away he could hear traffic sounds.

He felt so isolated and alone, he might as well have been on the moon.

He moved to the closet.

Closer.

Closer.

And put his hand on the doorknob, to turn it and yank the door open when—

He paused.

Shuddering.

What if he opened the door and his light shone not on a normal American teenager just having a good time for himself but a—

—monster of some sort?

What would the detective do then?

What good would his service revolver be?

Would anybody hear his shouts for help?

He listened.

Leaned toward the closet door.

And listened harder.

All he could hear was his own breath.

Coming in sweaty spasms.

He stared at the closet door.

What lurked inside there for him?

Would it jump out and rake his face before he even had a chance to defend himself?

And what if it was just a teenage kid and the detective got scared and overreacted and shot him?

No; he had to get a grip on himself.

Count to ten.

Breathe deeply.

Just the way they taught you to deal with stress at the academy.

Now.

Lean toward the door.

Extend your hand.

Put it on the knob.

Turn the knob and—

Fling the door open!

And—nothing.

He shone the flashlight around in the small confines of the walk-in closet. About all he could see was layer after layer of stained wallpaper that was peeling away.

He collapsed against the wall, laughing at his own fear.

A monster.

Right.

He kept on laughing, the sound echoing off the slanting walls of the closet.

He certainly wouldn't want to share this adventure with the other detectives back at the station.

Hey, did you hear about the monster a certain detective saw last night?

Those were the kind of stories detectives loved to tell about each other.

No, he'd be keeping all this to himself.

Especially as it turned out to be just his imagination.

But as he left the closet and started to walk out of the room, he turned around suddenly again.

Shining his light over the large, empty room.

He was positive that he'd followed something into this room.

A teenager, most likely.

But if so, where had the teenager gone?

The detective went over to the windows to see if they'd been opened.

Frost-rimmed, they were closed with nails and hadn't been opened for years.

So where had the teenager gone?

The detective went back into the closet and started looking around again. Seeing if there were any false bottoms or any false doors. Some of these old places had secret staircases that led from a closet to the bowels of the house.

The detective felt along every inch of closet wall.

Nothing.

Where had the teenager gone? Where?

Two years later Ed and Lorraine Warren accompanied the same detective plus a psychic photographer named Ethyl Whittaker to the old Phelps mansion.

Ed and Lorraine, who suspected from dozens of stories that the mansion was actually the sight of a demonic infestation, got the detective to agree only reluctantly.

Even after the passage of twenty-four months, the detective showed signs of real fear.

He still wasn't certain what he'd encountered in the darkness of the Phelps mansion, but he was now beginning to suspect that it had been nothing of human origin.

The detective was particularly reluctant to go upstairs. For a long time, he stood at the bottom of the staircase, looking up but not moving. Ed and Lorraine found this especially surprising because the man ordinarily displayed every sign of courage.

Ethyl Whittaker, the psychic photographer, had some good fortune that night. She was able to photograph a nunlike figure . . . much like the one reported by many of the area's residents.

As for the detective—

He finally went upstairs that night and obviously felt better for doing so. But he certainly didn't seem disappointed when they left the mansion once and for all.

According to Lorraine, "The Phelps mansion remains one of the most intriguing houses in all of New England.

"Several years after our investigation there, we heard a strange story from another policeman. He wrote us that he had retired from a nearby police department and had taken up repairing his house as a way of spending his days. One day he drove over to the Phelps mansion and took some bricks from out in back. He was planning to build a walkway to his garden in the rear of his house.

"He explained to us that ever since he had used the Phelps bricks, his life had changed—for the worse. Various accidents started happening around his house, for example. At first he refused to believe this had anything to do with the bricks.

"Being a former policeman, he was very skeptical of the supernatural. But along with the accidents, something else started happening. On some nights, out by the garden, he saw a nunlike figure leaning over the flower bed and then suddenly looking up at him as he stared at her.

"He was convinced he was having very real supernatural experiences."

Case File:

AMITYVILLE

An Interview with the Warrens

*FEW cases of the supernatural
are as misunderstood as the one involving the
Lutz family in Amityville. Because there has
been so much publicity surrounding the case,
many myths have been offered as fact.*

*During the course of our lectures, our
audiences inevitably bring up the subject, and
we take the time and patience to set the record
straight.*

We think it's fine that the topic continues to generate interest—as long as the truth is told.

—*Lorraine Warren*

Q: When we talk about the "Amityville horror" what, specifically, are we referring to?

Lorraine: Early in the morning of November 13, 1974, one of the sons of the DeFeo family took a high-powered rifle and killed the other six members of his family.

Q: That's the Amityville horror?

Lorraine: That and what followed when George and Kathleen Lutz moved in thirteen months after the murders occurred.

Q: The house had stood empty during that time?

Lorraine: Yes. Local people feared the house. Nobody wanted to buy it. There was a great deal of publicity surrounding the DeFeo murders, and the house acquired a grim reputation.

Q: Did some people feel that the DeFeo boy had been possessed when he'd killed his family?

Lorraine: Oh, yes, most definitely. As I said, there was a great deal of press about the tragedy, and invariably the stories started about demonic possession.

Q: The Lutzes didn't care about all this talk?

Lorraine: They didn't know about it. Not exactly, anyway. They were young and a good, strong family and I suppose the stories seemed silly to them.

Q: So they moved in?

Lorraine: Yes, they did, near Christmastime. Neither Ed nor I can testify firsthand to anything that happened in the Lutz house—we have to take Jay Anson's words for those events. He wrote the famous book about Amityville.

Q: The Lutzes had problems in the house?

Lorraine: Yes, and almost immediately.

Q: How would you characterize those problems?

Lorraine: Well, for one thing, both George and Kathleen experienced what psychologists call personality disintegration.

Ed: When you look through many of the cases we investigate, you see that during the course of demonic possession, a person begins to change. "Fred isn't himself anymore," we hear frequently. Or "Judy just doesn't normally do things like this." The loved ones of the possessed find it almost impossible to accept these behavioral changes. They can't imagine what could possibly change a person so profoundly.

Q: And you say this happened to the Lutzes?

Ed: George Lutz—again, all this is according to Jay Anson—went from a rock solid, hard-working man to a real slob given to volcanic shifts of temper.

Q: Was Kathleen Lutz affected?

Lorraine: Absolutely. Normally a very easygoing, pleasant person, she found herself turning angry for no reason she could see. It was as if something inside her were dictating her behavior.

Q: And things began happening in the house?

Lorraine: Jay Anson's theory seemed to be that

whatever demonic spirit had troubled the De-Feo boy was still loose in the house.

Q: So Anson was definitely convinced that the Lutzes were dealing with demonic possession?

Ed: In some respects, there could be no other explanation for what Anson claimed had happened.

Q: You seem cautious about Jay Anson's interpretation of the case.

Ed: My sense is that some things got dramatized beyond reality.

Q: Does this discredit the case?

Ed: Not at all.

Q: Then you think the Amityville horror took place as Anson suggested.

Ed: By and large. At least, his version of demonic infestation certainly squares with ours.

Q: In what way?

Ed: Well, look at the things the Lutzes reported. Hundreds of huge black flies appeared in the upstairs bedroom. The inside of the toilet bowls turned black, as if someone had painted them. A large statue moved around the house of its own volition. Windows opened and closed for no apparent reason.

Lorraine: Plus both George and Kathleen Lutz told of freezing temperatures that would not abate no matter how high they turned the heat—and then of sweltering heat that stayed with them no matter how many windows they opened.

Q: And you've experienced this with demonic infestation?

Ed: Oh, sure. Psychic cold, particularly.

Q: All this happened to the Lutzes over a short period of time, didn't it?

Ed: Yes; over a Christmas season.

Q: Then they moved?

Lorraine: Then they moved. Things had become pretty bad there.

Q: Worse than you've described so far?

Lorraine: Much worse. Kathleen was beginning to have dreams—nightmares, really—that involved the DeFeo family. They were quite vivid and quite disturbing.

Ed: Plus, the infestation itself had gotten worse.

Lorraine: A crucifix was turned upside down, for example, and that's almost always a sign that demons have begun to assert themselves.

Ed: And their children were beginning to be hurt. A boy got his hand crushed, though later there was no physical evidence of this. The demons were forcing family members to hallucinate, which, in some respects, can be the most frightening aspect of infestation.

Lorraine: And the Lutzes started to doubt their own sanity.

Ed: That's something we encounter very often.

Lorraine: We go into a house and interview the people and they tell us all sorts of things about what's been going on there—but rather than believe their own eyes and ears, they ask us if we think they're insane.

Ed: Most people in our society are trained to disbelieve in the demonic world.

Lorraine: Notice sometime how many laughs comedians get out of jokes about the demonic.

Ed: Most of us just don't want to deal with the demonic. Emotionally, we feel we can't. So we need to discredit it by saying that it's all imaginary.

Lorraine: It's easier for most people to think they're going insane than to deal with the possibility of demonic attack.

Ed: Psychologists call this denial, and we see this all the time. People just can't cope with the unknown.

Q: And that's what was going on with the Lutzes?

Ed: According to Anson, it was. And when you think about it, it's a natural reaction to stress. You don't want to admit what's really going on so you come up with a more comfortable explanation. "We've moved into a new house where something bad happened awhile back and we're just letting our imaginations run away with themselves." See? No real problem here. Nothing that good old reality can't handle.

Q: But they found out soon enough that "reality" couldn't explain what was going on?

Lorraine: Exactly.

Q: So where did that leave them?

Ed: Put yourself in their position. They're undergoing these radical transformations of personality—they've begun fighting with a viciousness that would have seemed impossible only a few weeks earlier—and all of a sudden doors are torn off their hinges and strange voices come

from empty rooms and the children are deeply
disturbed by it all.

Lorraine: So what do you do?

Ed: Ultimately they moved, of course, and that
was the sensible thing to do.

Q: Did it work? Was that the last of their demonic
infestation?

Ed: Apparently.

Q: You sound hesitant.

Ed: Well, moving isn't always a solution. We know
families who've moved into infested houses and
tried to move away—only to have the demons
follow them.

Q: That must be horrifying.

Lorraine: We know families who've fought this
kind of infestation for years.

Q: So what did the Lutzes conclude when they
left?

Lorraine: The impression we got from Jay Anson
was that they may have moved just in time.

Ed: What George, in particular, was concerned
about was that some member of the family—and
he certainly included himself as a possibility—
would do what the DeFeo boy did: pick up a
shotgun and kill everybody in the family.

Q: He felt that this was where the whole experience was leading?

Ed: Again, that's the impression we got.

Q: Do you think that was a real possibility?

Ed: Certainly.

Lorraine: Just because it happened once didn't

mean it couldn't happen again. George Lutz was probably right to worry about that.

Q: So there could have been another tragedy?

Ed: Easily. As we saw in The Devil in Connecticut case, where a young man who was possessed murdered his employer, demonic infestation often inclines a person to violence. And the problem is, you're never sure which person in a family will be overcome by this urge.

Lorraine: In the case of the DeFeos, for example, it was the son. Why not the father or mother?

Q: So if people find themselves in a circumstance similar to Amityville—where they're finding themselves changing personalities in unmistakable ways and where strange events are beginning to take place—what should they do?

Ed: Talk to their pastor as soon as possible. And if their pastor won't help them, find knowledgeable demonologists to assist them.

Lorraine: They're free to contact us too.

Q: But don't wait, is that what you're saying?

Ed: If you have legitimate reason to think that you or any of your family has come under the powers of the demonic, then the worst thing you can do is wait.

Q: That was a serious offer—they can contact you?

Lorraine: Sure. People contact us all the time.

Q: You think the Lutzes acted promptly, then?

Ed: Given all that had happened to them in so short a time, yes.

Lorraine: As soon as they became convinced that

there could be no other explanation for these events—they moved.

Q: Do books such as *The Exorcist* and *The Amityville Horror* help or hurt your cause?

Ed: The honest answer to that is "both." While they often overdramatize the demonic and risk having the public laugh instead of being curious enough to study the subject further, they do at least raise the topic in a sobering way.

Lorraine: *The Amityville Horror*, if nothing else, showed how a cursed house can affect very different families. And it showed how demonic infestation is a reality that can invade anyone's life.

Q: The Lutzes did seem like a pretty normal family.

Lorraine: Very normal. Very loving. And that's what made their experience all the more horrifying.

Case File:

THE HAUNTED VILLAGE

HAVING grown up in the same area as the town of Dudleytown, we'd often heard about the many strange occurrences that had supposedly taken place there.

Frankly, we were skeptical.

Ed and I turn down far more investigations than we take on for the simple reason that many "cases" aren't serious ones at all— but merely the stuff of rumor and gossip and innuendo. But so many people told us so many things about Dudleytown that ultimately we had no choice but to look into the matter.

—Lorraine Warren

New England is a land filled with the legends of ghosts and the supernatural. From the witches of Salem to Washington Irving's Headless Horseman, the states that comprise the original American colonies remain today the focus of occult activity that astonishes the world.

But even by New England's standards, the events that have taken place at Dudleytown over the past three centuries are remarkable.

And where do you find Dudleytown?

Well, though it no longer officially exists, you'll find its remains near Cornwall in Connecticut.

But before you learn of Dudleytown itself, consider the people who founded it.

In the England of the 1500s, there lived a man named Edmund Dudley who was minister to King Henry the Seventh and who also served as president of the King's Council. Not only was Dudley powerful, he was also, unfortunately for himself and his loved ones, treacherous.

Though Dudley was quite wealthy, his greed seemed to know no limits. He embezzled from the king's treasury and was punished by that most cruel of fates—beheading.

On August 18, 1510—a sweltering day in London—Edmund Dudley's head was severed from his body by the blow of a glistening ax.

Soon enough, other members of the Dudley clan found their way to the New World. Chief among them was Thomas Dudley, who despite Edmund's end was deputy governor of the prestigious and vitally important Massachusetts Bay Company, the real source of political authority among the colonists.

Not unlike Edmund, Thomas Dudley had a penchant for power and conniving. A Puritan of fanatical zeal, he imposed his own beliefs on all people under his control. Thomas Dudley despised Quakers. Under his command, members of that sect were tried for various crimes and executed with a nasty dispatch that made even their foes uneasy. Thomas Dudley gave every evidence of being a madman out of control.

During this time, it was said, one of the many men Dudley had put to death cursed not only the deputy governor but the entire area of Dudleytown, damning it forever.

After serving four different terms as full governor, a curious fate befell Thomas Dudley—he was found hacked to death in the area that would later come to be known as Dudleytown.

His killer was never found.

Shortly after this incident, four Dudley brothers, nephews of Thomas, discovered an area of wild land they felt strangely drawn to.

The brothers—Abijah, Bavzillai, Gideon, and Abviel—first saw this particular parcel of land on their return from the bloody French-Indian wars that had consumed the colonies for a decade.

They founded Dudleytown in 1632.

And almost immediately things started going wrong.

General Herman Swift, a Dudleytown resident, was away advising his superior officer George Washington, when his wife was struck by a bolt of lightning and killed. Shortly thereafter, General Swift went insane and had to be put away.

Dr. William Clark built a stately mansion on the edge of Dudleytown only to watch his wife slowly go mad as she was besieged by ghosts and terrible creatures that seemed to be half men, half beasts.

Mary Cheney married a prominent man who gave them both good advice. Her new husband, Horace Greeley, became known for saying "Go West, young man, go West!" Mary was only too happy to oblige. She found her Dudleytown upbringing to be frightening.

Year in and year out, Dudleytown men, women, and children were mysteriously killed—drowned, burned, clawed, poisoned, suffocated, bludgeoned—every vile and violent kind of death imaginable was visited on Dudleytown citizens.

Soon enough, throughout the 1800s, people began leaving Dudleytown.

Ghosts were frequently sighted, as were the half men, half beasts that had driven previous residents insane.

The once-prosperous township was now a ghost town but for one stubborn family. A man named Brophy scoffed at the idea that the place was cursed and declared his intentions to remain.

Then his wife died in a fall.

Then his children vanished, never to be seen again.

Then his house burned to the ground.

One rainy night Brophy stumbled into an inn in

the adjacent township, muttering madly of creatures with cloven hooves.

He was the last resident of Dudleytown. When he left, there were no more.

There is a story by the late horror writer H. P. Lovecraft that describes a once-beautiful valley suddenly and inexplicably ravaged—the crops dead, the trees naked and diseased, much of the land itself lost to a strange mist. Birdsong was no longer heard in the timbered hills nor could even moonlight make appealing the charred and ruined land.

It was as if the invisible hand of death had passed over the valley, rendering lifeless all it touched.

Over the fifty years following the expulsion of the pagans, something similar happened to Dudleytown. Indeed, a poet would, in 1884, describe the land as "very much like a moonscape as present-day science imagines such."

The poet, wandering on horseback through this singularly dreary tract of land, found little evidence of natural life anywhere. Oh, grass grew a pale green and tree limbs sprouted small buds, but for sound there was only the lonely wind and for sight only the arc of a lone blackbird flying high, as if afraid to touch down anywhere in this valley.

Dismounting, the poet climbed a rocky crag and looked full on at the valley below. There was evidence of a once-prosperous village, houses and out-buildings and a mill now in disrepair and empty, moss and lichen covering most of the rough timber.

On the frail wind, the poet imagined that he could hear the bright laughter of children on a summer day and of festive adults dancing in the evening. The music of lute and lyre seemed to fill the valley abruptly, and in the fallow fields there seemed to bloom corn and alfalfa and beans.

This must have been such a happy place once, the poet thought.

But now other sounds came to him on the wind, a dark laughter louder than any sound made by the festive villagers, a whisper of secrets known only to the elder pagan gods whose power extends through-out the cosmos.

In a vision, the poet saw babies die as they suckled, and husbands die as they loved wives, and innocent deer rendered by unseen forces. Similarly, he saw men flayed by the same unseen forces.

The older gods had been displeased by the Christians in the village, and so they had wrought their revenge—brought on by the curse of the Dudleys. . . .

No one lived there now.

Nothing of consequence grew there now.

There was just the wind and the faint smell of death.

Shuddering, the poet moved on, lest he too be tainted by the remarkable chill air of the place.

In the late 1930s, just before the onset of World War II, brave teenagers piled into their jalopies, big-band music blaring from their radios, and went to the highest hill of Dudleytown and proceeded to make out.

Half the thrill, as most of them realized, was the fact that it promised two great pleasures—sex and absolute terror.

Even the brave captain of the football team got so scared one night that he leapt from the convertible and ran back toward the main road—leaving his angry young girlfriend in the car.

What had he seen?

Or had he seen anything?

Nobody likes to fool himself and others more than a teenager. Perhaps the football captain started telling a story to scare his girlfriend—and woo her into his arms—when he got scared and took off running.

But if that was the case, then a lot of stories got told up there in the hills of Dudleytown, because over the years literally hundreds of stories were breathlessly told the local sheriff.

Stories about snout-faced creatures that materialized in a swirl of mist.

Stories about ear-deafening shrieks that were not quite human.

Stories about inhumanly cold hands that suddenly touched girls in their most secret places.

There was even a story about a seventeen-year-old boy who fought with some kind of monster deep in a ravine where he'd gone to relieve himself of the beer he and his girlfriend were drinking. All he could tell the sheriff was that the beast had eyes the color of blood and breath so foul the boy had to hold his own breath for much of the struggle.

Huge hands clawed the boy across the face, inflicting deep gashes, and then heavy footsteps could be heard running away through the thick, shadowy underbrush.

Shortly after this, the boy and his parents moved away, leaving no forwarding address whatsoever.

In 1983 the news staff of a nearby television station got what it considered a great idea for Dudleytown . What if the station sent a reporter up there on some dark night to do a report?

Well, despite a number of reservations about the idea, the station did in fact go ahead with the idea.

On a very dark night not long after, two expensive vans filled with television equipment rolled up the steep mountain leading to the top of Dudleytown.

Close behind bounced a new sedan carrying the attractive young female reporter and her favorite cameraman. Part of the setup included interviewing six parapsychology students who had been screened personally by Ed and Lorraine Warren.

Most of the TV people treated the whole experience as a lark—at least before they arrived on top of the mountain. There were a lot of Dracula and Frankenstein jokes and several of the grips made werewolf howls supposed to be partly scary and partly funny.

When they arrived there, circumstances changed abruptly.

The female reporter sensed something in the air of Dudleytown . . . a different quality, some sort of chill, to the air itself.

Even the darkness seemed to have a different texture, to be, well, *darker* than they were used to seeing.

And there were certain inexplicable odors . . .

Before she could begin her report, she became violently ill and had to be taken back to the car, unable to tape her story.

But it wouldn't have mattered anyway—most of the expensive equipment stored in the vans would not, for some mysterious reason, work. . . .

What was going on there?

The crew piled back into their vans and headed quickly back down the mountain.

"It's hard to say what's going on at Dudleytown," Lorraine Warren acknowledges today. "A great deal of it is the sort of myth-making people enjoy for its own sake. We all like scary stories, and Dudleytown is the perfect place to make up scary stories about.

"But the aspect of fun aside, when you're standing in the area, you really do sense some kind of . . . difference. Even in broad daylight, on a lovely summer afternoon, you see that things don't grow quite right there. And there's a strange silence to the place. You've never heard a place so *quiet*."

"We can't vouch for the stories of curses visited on Dudleytown early in its history," Ed says, "but even if there weren't demonic forces at work then . . . there certainly are now."

"Oh, yes, definitely," Lorraine agrees. "A few years ago a motorcycle gang started going to the mountain above Dudleytown and performing satanic rituals there. So by this time the place has been infested for sure."

Asked if he would spend a night on the mountain, Ed Warren says, "Sure I would if I thought it would serve a serious point, but at this time, I'm afraid too many people have been using the mountain and just inviting trouble. We'd just be in the way."

Lorraine adds, "What I'm afraid of is that with all the satanic rituals going on up there, something really horrible will happen."

Ed concludes, "All I know is that this is the classic situation—people toying with the idea of the demonic . . . and bringing on terrible trouble for themselves and their loved ones."

Case File:

THE PETRIFIED POLICEWOMAN

MANY people still labor under the false impression that psychic phenomena happens only to families that are somehow "different" from the norm. As the following study demonstrates, the supernatural imposes itself on the most average of families—and sometimes with terrifying results.

This story demonstrates that for many of us the occult is much closer by than we might realize.

—Ed Warren

Marie Bell was a very attractive mother of six. People were always surprised when she introduced herself as a policewoman. And not just a meter maid, but a real cop.

Marie and her husband, Phil, and their children lived in a rambling old New England–style frame house in Newtown, Connecticut, a town in which her family had lived for decades. The Bells were about as typical a family as you could find. Days were taken up with jobs and school, nights with activities that ranged from preparing tomorrow's lunches (Marie), to fixing cars (Phil), to doing homework and dating (the girls).

While the Bells had the usual complaints about life—they could always use a few extra dollars and there never seemed to be enough hours in the day to finish all their tasks—they were certainly a happy and contented family.

So when the strange events of that autumn began, they had no idea what to think.

Looking back, Marie became certain that the first things she became aware of were the sounds.

Tapping.

Phil said at once that the sounds were those of code, not unlike the Morse code.

But who would be tapping on their walls, and why?

At first, the Bells tried to dismiss the tapping as nothing to be concerned about. Didn't older homes often develop creaks and other noises that you couldn't explain?

During this time Marie read an article about Ed and Lorraine Warren. While she was interested in the piece, and even believed in the things the Warrens said, Marie didn't find the article relevant to anything she was experiencing.

At this point, she would have laughed if you'd tried to tell her that the supernatural was invading her life. She just wouldn't have believed you.

Something else was going on in Marie's life, something that was causing a certain anxiety.

Marie had been offered a job in Bethleham, New Hampshire, as head of security at a major hotel. The income would be approximately three times what she was making. The schools there were good and the housing situation was favorable to buyers. Phil was all for the move. He saw opportunities for himself there too.

So what stopped them?

Well, Marie was reluctant to leave a house that had been in the family since the 1930s.

One day she was ready to pick up and go to Bethleham, the next she became anxious and decided she wouldn't go.

Phil found Marie's indecision mildly alarming. Usually Marie just made up her mind and then acted on her decision. No looking back, no second-guessing.

She just did it.

So why wouldn't she move to Bethleham?

Shortly after the tapping began, she began having dreams of her grandfather, Richard Jeremiah Stanton.

While she had loved the old man—she had grown up around him—she hadn't dreamed of him so vividly in years.

In the dreams, he said nothing to her. But she had the impression that he was deeply unhappy about something.

But what?

Richard Jeremiah Stanton had been a beloved and memorable character in local affairs. A huge man who had been born in a covered wagon in the Badlands, he had run away to sea at fourteen, serving aboard whaling ships and trawlers, and at thirty-two had come back to the States where he had built the fine family home that he wanted the Stantons to live in for generations.

He had become a local celebrity when he announced, on the day the home was completed, that he wanted the house to always be a "port in the storm" for any Stanton.

But he went this kind of dedication even one better by saying that he would "haunt any Stanton who tried to give up the house."

He had lived out his long life raising a family, working around the house, and telling stories of his days and nights at sea.

He was well regarded in his community, and when he passed on he was genuinely mourned.

At the time that Marie Bell was talking about moving from the family house, she had no idea that her grandfather's curse had come true. She had no idea that her grandfather was now haunting her.

Marie wasn't sure where the idea came from.

But whatever its source, it proved persistent. Marie thought of contacting the Warrens.

From a radio show, she learned that they would be appearing at a nearby college and that their presentation would be open to the public.

Marie sat up most of a night debating whether or not to go.

On the one hand, the knocking had gotten much worse. Almost certainly, it was some kind of code—but what kind and what was its purpose?

And who was sending the code?

On the other hand, Marie felt the New Englander's reluctance to make your personal problems public.

Surely people would whisper about her.

Surely people would snicker.

They'd probably snicker at the whole family, should the rapping ever become public knowledge.

Toward dawn, Marie fell asleep.

When the sky had turned a pearl color—just before the sun erupted in red fire behind the heavy gray clouds—Marie thought she'd heard a voice.

Calling her name.

Stirring from bed, she got up, tugged on her robe, and stood in the center of the floor.

Faintly, she could hear the tapping once more.

What was it saying?

While she was fixing breakfast, she made up her mind.

She was going to see the Warrens.

The hall where the Warrens spoke that night was crowded. Eager students and faculty alike paid total attention to the couple at the front of the room who detailed their lives as demonologists through slides and audio tapes.

The air was excited, electric.

Marie slipped into a seat at the rear.

Any doubt she might have had about the Warrens were soon banished forever. The couple spoke in direct, sincere, and nondramatic words about the other realm known as the supernatural.

They offered examples that both startled and reassured—startled because some of their tales were frightening; reassured because here was proof positive that life goes on beyond our time on earth.

At the end, the students and faculty rose and gave the Warrens a very warm salute for their efforts that evening.

Lorraine, looking over the shoulders and heads of the students who surrounded her afterward, caught sight of a shy, attractive woman in the rear of the hall.

Lorraine wondered who the woman was.

What her purpose there was.

Lorraine sensed that the woman desperately wanted to talk but, for some reason, was afraid to.

Finally, as the students dispersed, the woman approached Lorraine and introduced herself. She stated her problem with a great deal of difficulty.

Lorraine could see that Marie Bell was not the type of woman often given to imposing her problems on strangers.

Lorraine brought Ed over and for the next half hour they talked, after which Ed and Lorraine agreed to go to the Bell house soon.

Lorraine had been having dreams lately herself. One dream was especially troubling. She was in an automobile with a low roof. The automobile was struck from behind. Lorraine was injured.

Lorraine couldn't imagine how this could happen.

Ed always drove whenever they went anywhere.

So why would a woman be driving? And where did the car with the low roof come from?

Lorraine soon had her answer.

A few days later Ruth Ann Devlin, a reporter with a local newspaper, joined Ed and Lorraine and a psychic photographer in exploring a house that was supposedly haunted.

Ruth and Lorraine followed Ed in his car.

Halfway to their destination, a drunken driver struck Ruth and Lorraine from behind.

Lorraine was seriously injured and was taken to the hospital. She saw now that her dream had been prophetic.

When she got out of the hospital, Lorraine found that two things had happened to her—she was wearing a neck brace . . . and her psychic powers had increased.

Injury, as the psychic Edgar Cayce had known, often increased one's mental abilities . . . particularly if one was psychically gifted already.

Lorraine was to find out just how helpful this injury would be.

Two days later, on the way to the Bell house, Lorraine began receiving fleeting psychic pictures of a large, blustery seafaring man with white hair and outsize features. She knew this to be Richard Jeremiah Stanton, Marie Bell's grandfather.

The closer the Warrens got to the Bell house, the more vivid the images became.

Terrifyingly so.

While the Warrens were approaching, the Bells were spending a typical night.

Phil was in the garage working on a car. The girls were in various places at home and around the town. And the littlest child, Tinker, was helping her mother with sewing and some occasional TV viewing.

Around nine, Marie and Tinker were on the bed upstairs when they heard a terrible crash.

Flying downstairs, Marie found her best china

shattered all over the kitchen floor, china that had been her mother's.

Back upstairs, trying to calm down, Marie took Tinker in her arms and closed her eyes. Then a massive sound startled her.

Half hysterical, Marie ran downstairs to see if everything was all right.

She found more china smashed on the floor. And the family butcher knife stuck deep into the wood-work . . . as if it had been thrown to hurt someone.

Or kill him.

Tinker began shouting from the vestibule.

On the stairs was a luminous form, vaguely man-shaped, coming down the stairs.

The form was nearly blinding to look on.

Marie had scarcely gotten to Tinker, when she began hearing more crashing sounds from another part of the house.

In the living room, a brass ashtray—which had belonged to Richard Jeremiah Stanton—was flying around the room smashing things.

Including a photograph of Stanton himself.

What Marie Bell was looking at was a glimpse of hell.

By the time the Warrens arrived, the Bells were terribly upset. Ed and Lorraine were as reassuring as possible, asking to see where the damage had been done, asking them to repeat exactly what had been happening not only that evening but over the past few months.

Marie led the Warrens through the house. It was then that Lorraine began seeing an image of an apple tree and a little girl in a swing. The girl wore white stockings, long curls, and pink ribbons.

The swing was being pushed by a tall man.

Lorraine recognized him as Stanton.

Lorraine, who was relating her vision to Ed, sat down on a chair. Ed asked if the vision could provide them proof that it was real.

"Upstairs in a crawlspace," a voice told Lorraine.

The Bells and the Warrens went upstairs and began looking through the crawlspace.

After fifteen minutes they found a dusty shoe box.

After opening it up, they discovered photos of Stanton's funeral plus various pictures of Stanton throughout his lifetime. One newspaper clipping was dated 1937.

They took the box downstairs and went through the box for closer inspection.

Marie began to understand that her grandfather's motives weren't sinister at all. He was merely trying to protect his family from the unknown, obviously believing that nothing terrible would befall them if they stayed there, in the family home.

Marie, who did plan to leave for her new job, felt much better about this revelation.

But the case didn't end there.

When they reached home late that night, the Warrens went into their study to look for a letter Ed had received that morning.

What they found instead was an obituary sitting right on the desk—the obituary of Stanton himself.

Sent there by supernatural means to let Ed and Lorraine know that they had indeed been in contact with a seafaring ghost.

Lorraine says, "The Bells were such a nice family, we were happy that they saw how much Marie's grandfather loved them all and how protective he was.

"Eventually, my neck brace came off and most of my aches and pains went away. While I lost none of my powers, I did lose some of the intensity that accompanied my visions during this period. I don't think it would be worth nearly breaking my neck to recover them again, however."

Case File:

A POLTERGEIST EXPLOSION

An Interview with Ed Warren

MANY readers will know the "Lindley Street Infestation" simply because it is perhaps the most widely reported case involving a poltergeist in the past few decades.

Ed and I are still asked many questions about Lindley Street and the people who lived there and what became of them. Discussing it is a mixed bag for us. There are moments of great joy, certainly, but there are also moments of sorrow.

But whatever our feelings about the case, it made thousands of converts to our cause.

*And was extremely useful in recruiting serious
young demonologists to help us out with our
investigations.*

—Lorraine Warren

Q: When did you first learn about Lindley Street?
Ed: Our good friend Mary was keeping tabs on the
case as it was developing. We hadn't been ap-
prised of it. In fact, we were just wrapping up a
very intense investigation and battling some
personal problems. My mother had just passed
away and I was, needless to say, feeling her loss.
Lorraine was getting the house ready for visitors. Many of my mother's friends were coming
over to our place for a gathering.
Q: That was when Mary called?
Ed: Right. Mary's not very excitable but—
Q: —but she was that day?
Ed: (*Smiles*) Very excited. I could imagine her
jumping up and down at the end of the phone.
And I didn't blame her. People who devote their
lives to the occult pray that someday a case will
come along that is so clear-cut, even the great-
est doubter will have to believe. We're used to
scorn and disbelief and all sorts of insults about
our sanity and our motives.
Q: And the case Mary was describing was one of
those clear-cut examples?
Ed: Very much so. In fact, I couldn't think of an
example to equal it in the past twenty or thirty
years.

Q: What was she describing?

Ed: Well, she said that on Lindley Street in Bridgeport, Connecticut, policemen, priests, and reporters were all seeing manifestations of poltergeists.

Q: And they were acknowledging they were seeing these things?

Ed: Oh, yes. Mary said that the story was all over the air and that we should get down there and see for ourselves what was going on.

Q: So Mary didn't seem to be exaggerating?

Ed: Not at all.

Q: Did you leave right away?

Ed: As soon as I could.

Q: Did Lorraine go along?

Ed: She came later.

Q: So you went alone?

Ed: Yes.

Q: Were you excited?

Ed: (*Laughs*) Shaking, literally. I wanted to find a situation that was as clear-cut as Mary said it was going to be. I suppose I was also grateful to the situation for another reason.

Q: Oh?

Ed: Whenever you suffer a personal loss such as I had—you know, my mother dying—you're grateful for events that distract you for a time from your sorrow.

Q: I see.

Ed: I'd been very close to my mother, but the events on Lindley Street promised a respite.

Q: Did you break the speed limit getting there?

Ed: (*Laughs*) Just about.

Q: Had you been to Bridgeport before?

Ed: Many times. It's a beautiful city, as you know. But I wasn't prepared at all for what I saw.

Q: And that was?

Ed: Well, Mary had told me to look for St. Vincent's Hospital and I did. She said that Lindley Street was nearby. She said that the hospital would point me in the right direction.

Q: Did it?

Ed: I didn't need the hospital.

Q: You didn't?

Ed: No. There were so many people around the Goodin home—Gerald and Laura Goodin were the couple experiencing the demonic infestation—that you couldn't have missed the place if you'd wanted to.

Q: How many people do you suppose were there?

Ed: There were about three police cars, two fire department vehicles, and about thirty-five people. It did not build up to ten or fifteen thousand until about the third day, when it became a top international news story. Fifteen hundred people at least. I'll never forget the sensation. I was coming up over the rise of the hill and then down below me were all these people swarming around. It was as if it were the end of the world and this one small house was the only place left with any food.

Q: What did you do?

Ed: Needless to say, I had to park at some distance and then I had to work my way through the crowd. People were screaming and shouting and pointing. There was something almost frightening about it. You sensed that this was a crowd that could very easily get out of control.

Q: Were you afraid?

Ed: Concerned maybe, not afraid.

Q: Did you think of turning back?

Ed: I suppose the thought crossed my mind.

Q: Did anybody hassle you in any way?

Ed: No; as I said, it was just that everything was at such a fever pitch, I had to wonder what was going to happen. I even saw a few people crying. All I could think of were the stories you heard about Lourdes. How people break into tears and wailing as they reach the waters. It was sort of like that.

Q: How did you eventually wind up at the house?

Ed: I told two police officers who I was and explained to them that I was there for a very serious purpose. Fortunately, they believed me.

Q: So you were taken to the house?

Ed: Yes.

Q: And were permitted inside?

Ed: Yes, once they knew who I was.

Q: What was it like inside?

Ed: A mess. Unlike anything I'd ever seen.

Q: In what way?

Ed: Well, every few minutes something would get tipped over or knocked over or torn from the wall. This had been going on for some time, so you could imagine what the place looked like.

Q: And there were witnesses to all this?

Ed: Oh, yes. That's what made the Lindley Street

case so extraordinary. For one of the first times, you had a good dozen witnesses.

Q: Such as—

Ed: Such as policemen, to start with.

Q: Why were policemen there?

Ed: Well, one of the Goodins' neighbors was a Bridgeport officer named Holdsworth.

Q: How did he get involved?

Ed: He was walking home when the Goodins called him. They'd heard noises. There is no upstairs, it is a one-story building.

Q: So he came in to investigate?

Ed: Right.

Q: And what did he find?

Ed: Well, he came in and told them to wait on the little sunporch. Holdsworth goes into the kitchen. The noises are even clearer. But that wasn't what really startled him.

Q: He heard something else?

Ed: No, he came and walked toward the kitchen and there he saw the refrigerator teetering back and forth and it bumped him in the elbow.

Q: And he had no doubt he saw this?

Ed: No doubt at all.

Q: What did he do?

Ed: Well, after he searched the house for an explanation, he then got the Bridgeport police involved, and the Goodins tried to get their local parish involved.

Q: The Goodins didn't have any luck?

Ed: The Catholic church shies away from any kind

of publicity. From that standpoint, this case was no different.

Q: So they wouldn't cooperate at all?

Ed: Not "at all." They did send a very nice priest who blessed the house and blessed everybody in it. That was quite a moving scene, as a matter of fact. You had the Goodin family and all these uniformed officers kneeling on the floor and the priest was blessing them.

Q: Did the poltergeist explosion continue?

Ed: Oh, yes.

Q: So you saw some of it firsthand?

Ed: Not only saw it but was involved with it.

Q: Did Lorraine join you?

Ed: Yes, she came over with Father Bill Charbonneau, a priest from our area who studied in Rome and who is a researcher and who was then teaching a course in the occult including parapsychology.

Q: What did they make of what they saw?

Ed: First of all, by the time they got there, the crowd outside the house was even larger. Some reports put it at ten thousand.

Q: Was the world press involved?

Ed: Yes, by this time all three American networks were there as well as journalists from virtually every country. It was called the most important news story for that entire forty-eight-hour period.

Q: Had things settled down inside the house?

Ed: They had settled down to this degree—Father Charbonneau assessed things and then talked over his impressions with us and then decided to spend some time with the nine-year-old Goodin girl.

Q: Did Father Charbonneau find something special about her?

Ed: Well, in investigations such as ours, you're always looking for conduits—ways that the demonic get into households. Demons often use children.

Q: So Father Charbonneau was thinking that perhaps demons had used her?

Ed: Perhaps.

Q: Was there something different about her?

Ed: The Goodins had lost their only child, a son. He'd been very young and had died terribly. After his death, they adopted this young Seven Nations Indian girl from Canada. They loved her very much right from the outset but certainly they had to admit there were certain problems. At school, for example, some of the other children teased her and taunted her. As a result of this, it would only be natural for her to become an insular child. I suppose she may have developed a rich fantasy life, the way lonely children often do. When she was at home she seemed happy, but outside the home the adjustment problems continued.

Q: Did she play any part in the events during this forty-eight-hour period?

Ed: The Goodins told us a strange story about her cat. The cat was named Sam, and it seemed that he talked. At least that was the impression you could get. You'd be standing in an empty room with Sam beside you and you'd hear this voice and you'd look down and the only possible source of the voice would be Sam. Well, since Father Charbonneau had trained at Pontifical University in Rome and was well acquainted with demonology, he knew about such cats. Then he decided to spend some time interviewing the girl.

Q: Did the cat talk?

Ed: What Father Charbonneau learned was that the Goodins were the victims of a "poltergeist attack." It wasn't the cat talking—or singing "Jingle Bells"—it was a case of demons trying to rattle people by making the cat appear to converse.

Q: Hadn't there been a case of this with the girl's tutor?

Ed: Yes. At some point the Goodins thought it would be a good idea to hire a tutor for their daughter. A very nice woman began giving her lessons. One day they heard this really foul cursing and swearing coming from behind a closed door. It was this voice demanding that the door be opened. When they opened the door, all they found was the cat. They checked everywhere to make sure that there wasn't somebody hiding somewhere—but no. The only possible source for the sound was Sam, the cat. Needless to say, the tutor was shaken by this. The Goodins had a very difficult time persuading her to come back.

Q: Did she ever go back?

Ed: I don't think so. This was about the time when strange things started happening to the Goodins consistently—and people pick up on this, sense it, and start shying away.

Q: When were the Goodins convinced that the supernatural was involved?

Ed: I'm not sure which incident triggered it exactly, but certainly one of the most frightening events happened in their own kitchen.

Q: This was near the time when the police were called in?

Ed: This happened the Saturday night before Ed was called in.

Q: What happened?

Ed: Laura Goodin was at the stove making dinner. Her husband and daughter were at the table. The Goodins have a large console floor-model TV in the kitchen next to the stove so they can watch the news when they're eating. Anyway, Laura Goodin was making dinner and all of a sudden this very heavy TV set was lifted up by no power the Goodins could see—and came over and dropped on Laura's foot.

Q: Was she injured?

Ed: Two toes were broken.

Q: What did they do?

Ed: At this point, they weren't sure what to do. Many people in these circumstances are afraid to do anything.

Q: Afraid they'll be seen as crazy?

Ed: Or mercenary in some way—as if they've made it all up for some personal reason.

Q: Are there places people in these circumstances can turn?

Ed: (*Laughs*) Well, Lorraine and I can always be contacted.

Q: Does it help for people to contact their church or parish?

Ed: Sometimes. Though I have to say, the clergy can be among the most skeptical of all people. Even downright cruel at times. I'm certainly not suggesting that all clergy are this way—or even close to a majority of clergy—but I say this as a cautionary. You will occasionally find priests and ministers and rabbis who are almost antagonistic when you bring up the subject of the supernatural.

Q: But the day Father Charbonneau spent interviewing the girl he wasn't hostile at all?

Ed: Not at all. He wanted to learn what was going on in the house.

Q: What did he discover?

Ed: Well, again, it's the classic problem. Troubled children attract the demonic.

Q: And she sounded troubled to you?

Ed: Sure. If nothing else, there was what she went through at school. You know, for all our supposed tolerance as Americans, we still have a difficult time accepting people from foreign countries as neighbors. And it was as simple as that with her.

Q: But she didn't invite the demonic into her life?

Ed: Oh, no; nothing like that. She may have been the simple conduit.

Q: May have been?

Ed: We didn't have time to do anything definitive during that very chaotic forty-eight hours.

Q: So even after Father Charbonneau spoke with her, strange events continued to take place?

Ed: Well, for just one example, Lorraine's hand was burned very severely when she was just sitting in a chair. I've rarely seen Lorraine in that much pain. It was a psychic burn, meaning that it was inflicted by the demonic. (*Smiles*) And there was even one sort of funny incident. There was this table that just went up in the air every so often. It would fly around the room and then settle back down. I was standing in the room where the table was when I saw this woman coming through the kitchen with an urn of coffee. Obviously she was going to set this down on the table. I stopped her just in time before she set the urn down. And just as I did so, the table picked up and started somersaulting in the air again. If the urn had been on it, there would have been scalding coffee everywhere. That's one thing about a situation like this— there are moments that are really comic.

Q: How were the police during all this?

Ed: Over the years, we've worked with some really fine, cooperative officers, but I don't think we've ever met a group that matched this one for sheer stamina. They were fascinated and a little bit afraid of what was going on—but they stayed right there, helping out in every way they could.

Q: So they were directly involved in some of the events?

Ed: Sure. Such as the TV sets that would raise up from their tables and set down very swiftly on the floor. They would move in such a way that they wouldn't break but they would just keep smashing to the floor.

Q: What were the crowds outside like by this time?

Ed: The world press estimates were saying that the crowds now exceeded more than ten thousand. The story that seemed to excite them particularly—draw even more people to the area—was the exploding crucifix.

Q: That happened the second day?

Ed: Actually, it happened both days. But people everywhere sensed the significance of it. When you think about it a moment, that's the ultimate act of defilement. The body of Christ on the cross—representing the very moment he died for our sins—and this is exploded. Obviously, the demonic forces are telling us something.

Q: What do you think they're telling us?

Ed: That they want chaos to win. (*Leans forward*) Look, there are two primal forces at work in the cosmos. Chaos and order. Chaos is illness, madness, suffering, hatred, war. Those are just a few of the things chaos inspires. Order is love, compassion, creativity, optimism. These were the things Jesus Christ inspired in all of us. Chaos wants to destroy the good human impulses and replace them with— Well, take an area like the Middle East. You can see chaos working there, and it's been that way in that area since before the time of Christ. That's what happens when we don't hold on to our beliefs, when we let our darkest impulses overtake us.

Q: So you were seeing all this at the Goodin home?

Ed: Absolutely. For example, a seminarian came on the second day and led the family in a rosary. Some of the Goodin family joined in. It was a very religious, very touching moment. But as the seminarian was finishing, a black form appeared and punched him. He knew what the foggy, dark form was, of course—and he picked up the girl in his arms and carried her out of the house.

Q: So she was safe?

Ed: The form followed him as he ran to the next door neighbor's.

Q: But he eluded it?

Ed: Yes. He was shaken, as was the girl, of course, but it followed him to the house, and pounded on the door.

Q: And back at the home—

Ed: Back at the home, the biggest poltergeist explosion we've ever seen continued.

Q: Objects were flying around—

Ed: —and furniture upended—

Q: —and rappings were in the wall—

Ed: —and voices were heard in closets and walkways and— (*Shakes his head*) Again, I've never seen anything like it.

Q: How were the Goodins bearing up?

Ed: All things considered, very well.

Q: How were you and Lorraine bearing up?

Ed: As I've told you, we'd just had a death in the family so we were emotionally fatigued. By the end of the second day, we really needed to get back to some sort of normalcy.

Q: Meaning what?

Ed: (*Laughs*) Meaning showers, meals, clean clothes—that sort of thing.

Q: So you'd gotten back to normalcy as you say and—

Ed: —and the phone rang.

Q: This was Father Charbonneau, correct?

Ed: Correct.

Q: And he said what?

Ed: (*Sighs*) He said that the Bridgeport chief of police had pronounced the whole thing on Lindley Street a hoax.

Q: How could he do that—when so many witnesses, including his own men, would testify to what they'd seen?

Ed: We've never been sure. The police can do anything in the name of law and order. Apparently, most of the blame was put on the girl. According to the Chief, she was behind the hoax.

Q: Did the Goodins go along with this?

Ed: Not really. They did not agree that their daughter was responsible for the incident although they didn't accept a supernatural cause, either. Here was what amounted to a miracle—

positive proof of the other regions we've dedicated our lives to exploring—and it was all being negated.

Q: But you don't know why?

Ed: (*Sighs*) The usual reasons, I suppose.

Q: Those being?

Ed: Most of us just don't want to face the supernatural. And that's always struck me as strange. Here we are, a nation that seems to believe deeply in some sort of life beyond this one, yet we don't want to believe that that life might have any effect on our current existence. Here's this entire other realm—the supernatural, for want of a broader term—and we want to do everything to deny it. Most people get embarrassed when you bring the subject up—yet these are the same people who go to church every Sunday and pray to a God most of them have never seen nor spoken with. If we can imagine—and believe in—a godhead, then what's so difficult about accepting God's opposite . . . the darker realm's?

Q: Have you kept in touch with the Goodins?

Ed: No.

Q: With Father Charbonneau?

Ed: Oh, sure. We speak with him frequently. And work with him.

Q: Any regrets about the Lindley Street case?

Ed: I suppose. I mean, it would have been nice—in retrospect—to have our own independent witnesses. People who could have given irrefutable testimony to what went on there those two days.

Q: You sound almost angry.

Ed: (*Sighs*) It just seems a waste. Fortunately, one thing came from all the events.

Q: What's that?

Ed: Independent documentation by various police officers who were there during most of these events.

Q: You have their written versions of events?

Ed: Yes, we do. And we feel it vindicates our version of the events.

SOME
FINAL
THOUGHTS

AS you've learned by now, our investigations into psychic and supernatural phenomena have taken us all over the world. Into several worlds, really, when you consider the nature of our endeavors.

For those of you who have experienced troubling phenomena, we urge you not to be afraid. Contact any serious demonologist in your area. Or contact a sympathetic member of the clergy.

But above all, don't lose faith.

During our decades as demonologists, we've learned that faith alone remains the single most powerful weapon in battling the dark forces. Without faith, there is little hope that you will be able to withstand the temptations and the griefs demons often inflict on human beings.

In the course of reading this book, you have seen virtually every sort of human being do battle with the supernatural. In some cases, as in the West Point story, the demons were relatively benign.

But when you think of the young woman who ended up in a psychiatric hospital—or the terrified villagers who came in contact with Bigfoot—then you realize that many cases of the supernatural are not benign at all but are instead dangerous and occasionally even fatal.

Faith.

It's the only solution.

If you're currently wondering about a situation in your own life—small but troubling events that seem to portend an encounter with the dark forces—educate yourself as well as possible.

Seek out books that offer wisdom on the subject, not books that offer only sensationalism and hysteria.

Lorraine and I will continue to take our message to every corner of the world. In the next year alone, we'll be visiting many places we've never been before.

Along with us we'll take the goodwill, the sincerity, and the deep religious faith so many of you have offered us over the years.

While our lives are occasionally frightening, they are also rewarding because so many of you have allowed us to help you. Through God's abiding will, we have a more mature and sophisticated understanding of what is really going on in this world we call earth.

—Ed Warren

All Futura Books are available at your bookshop or newsagent, or can be ordered from the following address:

    Futura Books,
    Cash Sales Department,
    P.O. Box 11,
    Falmouth,
    Cornwall TR10 9EN.

Alternatively you may fax your order to the above address. Fax No. 0326 376423.

Payments can be made as follows: Cheque, postal order (payable to Macdonald & Co (Publishers) Ltd) or by credit cards, Visa/Access. Do not send cash or currency. UK customers: please send a cheque or postal order (no currency) and allow 80p for postage and packing for the first book plus 20p for each additional book up to a maximum charge of £2.00.

B.F.P.O. customers please allow 80p for the first book plus 20p for each additional book.

Overseas customers including Ireland, please allow £1.50 for postage and packing for the first book, £1.00 for the second book, and 30p for each additional book.

NAME (Block Letters) ....

ADDRESS ....

....

☐ I enclose my remittance for _____

☐ I wish to pay by Access/Visa Card

Number ☐☐☐☐☐☐☐☐☐☐☐☐☐☐☐☐

Card Expiry Date ☐☐☐☐